BADMINTON
everyone

M.B. Chafin
University of Florida

M. Malissa Turner
Southeastern Louisiana University

ᕼᵀᵢ Hunter Textbooks Inc.

Consulting Editor: Dr. Clancy Moore, University of Florida

Copyright 1984 by Hunter Textbooks Inc.

ISBN 0-88725-013-0

Inquiries regarding this book or others in this series should be addressed to:

Hunter Textbooks Inc.
823 Reynolda Road
Winston-Salem, North Carolina 27104

CONTENTS

ACKNOWLEDGMENTS

The authors would like to express appreciation to several individuals who assisted in the preparation of this book. For their assistance in providing photographs, special thanks to Dr. Robert Kelly and his advanced badminton students at Southeastern Louisiana University — Joe Jones, Deirdre Bailey, Ricky Creel, and Tommy Krysan — and at the University of Florida, to Eric Sauerberg, Jeane Lucas, Thomas Soepardi, Brian Woloscheck, and Mike Chafin. Jim McCachren provided valuable assistance in the preparation of skills tests and Charley Davis and Eleanor Delaney are commended for their assistance in preparing the manuscript.

Chapter 1

Values of Badminton

Welcome to the wonderful world of badminton, the sport with the unique projectile! The shuttlecock (commonly called a shuttle, bird, or birdie) is largely responsible for making badminton the fascinating and enjoyable sport that it is. The conical design with its unique feather construction creates a projectile capable of an unusual variety of speeds. Air resistance quickly decelerates the hardest hit and the shuttle's easy response to gentle amounts of force lends itself to many techniques. Beginners quickly achieve success and enjoyment, while advanced players find sufficient challenge to last a lifetime. All ages can play badminton because the lightness of the shuttle and racket requires minimal strength.

Physical conditioning can be achieved through badminton play when rallies are long and require great court movement. Aerobics benefits from singles play between skilled opponents are equal to or greater than that of tennis, skating or volleyball for similar amounts of time. Stretching and lunging to hit shuttles which are just out of reach develop flexibility of the hips, thighs, and shoulders, while agility is improved by the accelerated movements players are required to make on the court. Improved eye-hand coordination is another prominent outcome of badminton play.

Psychological benefits of the game are many — including enhanced self-concept, competition, and stress reduction. Participants who may have had difficulty finding a sport they could play usually become more confident and assured. The thrill of competition can be experienced by all players at any level and a fast-paced game or match can greatly dissipate the anxiety and tension accumulated during a stressful day.

Badminton also stimulates high levels of intellectual activity. Mental agility involving strategy of play may win as many points at all levels of competition as physical skills. This is the reason why some champions have retained their top ranking for years. As an example, Mrs. R. C. Tragett was able to win the All-England Singles Championship in 1912 and again in 1928. She also won the Doubles Championships in 1908 and 1926. One thing is certain, badminton does encourage the skills of thinking quickly and planning ahead. Doubles play can be as challenging as singles and provides great

Mixed doubles is a challenging game and a popular social activity.

opportunities for developing cooperation between partners. Regular doubles and mixed doubles are popular social outlets for participants of all ages.

Badminton is an inexpensive sport. Basic equipment is moderately priced and the court is relatively small and easy to construct. Since badminton can be played indoors or outdoors, it has an advantage over other sports which must be played in a particular location requiring large areas of space.

Origin of the Game

The history of badminton is as interesting as the game itself. Tracing the acts of its origins is almost as mysterious and intriguing as the anticipation of the flight of the shuttle by a novice player. The earliest game using a shuttle-like object was played in China more than 2000 years ago. A children's game called "battledore and shuttlecock" was played in Europe between the eleventh and fourteenth century. This game was described as hitting a strangely-shaped object with a "batedor" (translated as an instrument for beating).

Based on pictorial evidence, a badminton-like game was thought to have been played in Poland in the late seventeenth and eighteenth centuries. A portrait, "Young Prince Sulkowski" by Adam Manyoki, portrays a young man of the royal family of Poland holding a shuttlecock and racket.

A game called "poona," originated and played in India in the 1870s, was also a forerunner of badminton. One story (which may or may not be true) suggests that British officers on duty in Poona, India, after consuming the contents of a bottle, attached feathers to the cork and began hitting this "homemade" shuttle back and forth.

The game was first called badminton in the middle of the nineteenth century (1873) when it was played at Badminton, the country estate of the Duke of Beaufort in Gloucestershire, England. The timing of this event was so close to the origin of poona that some authorities suggest that poona was an off-shoot of badminton while others claim badminton was a derivative of poona. British army officers are generally given credit for playing each game for the first time at both locations — England as well as India. The Duke of Beaufort's house was responsible for a unique feature of the early playing area for badminton. The game was played in a hall which had doors opening inward at each end of the net, to allow room for spectators to enter and leave the room without disturbing play. Another interesting feature was that the court was much narrower at the net than at the two ends of the court, thus creating an hourglass shape. This shape persisted until 1901 when the present dimensions were established. Other rules formalized in 1877 were revised about 1890, and have changed only slightly since that time.

Two British players, Bayard Clark and E. Langdon (Landon) Wilkes, introduced badminton to the United States and formed an exclusive organization, the Badminton Club of New York, in the winter of 1878-1879. Though more social than athletic in nature, this club is recognized as the oldest badminton club (having continuous existence) in the world.

The Badminton Association of England, the first national organization for badminton, was established by a few local clubs in 1893 for the purpose of promoting badminton play nationally and internationally. The first All-England Championship was held in 1897. This tournament is presently held annually and is considered to be one of the most prestigious.

The United States organization came into existence in 1936 and organized its first national championship in 1937 and its first junior nationals in 1947. First established as the American Badminton Association, it is now called the United States Badminton Association (USBA).

International matches have been played since 1902 when Ireland played a team from England although the International Badminton Federation (IBF) was not formed until 1934. World Championships were begun in 1948-1949 when the United States and nine other nations competed for the Thomas Cup — a championship fashioned in the manner of the prestigious Davis Cup for tennis. The United States won the first match in this inaugural championship by defeating Canada but eventually lost to Malaysia, the team ultimately winning the title "Champion Nation" and the Thomas Cup, named for Sir George Thomas. This Championship is held every three years.

The Uber Cup, the women's version of the Thomas Cup, was first initiated in 1957. The cup was donated by Mrs. H. S. Uber, an outstanding mixed doubles player. The United States was successful in winning the first three championships. This championship, sponsored by the Ladies International Badminton Championship, is held every three years.

It is generally acknowledged that the best world players come from the Far East. In Malaysia, Indonesia, and Thailand, badminton has the status of a national game. The Thomas Cup championships have been won consistently by Indonesia and Malaysia while the Uber Cup matches have been dominated by Japan and Indonesia.

Name_____

Chapter 1 Evaluation

1. What is responsible for the unique features of the game of badminton?

2. List the major physiological, psychological, intellectual and social benefits to be derived from badminton play.

3. Name two predecessors of badminton and their countries of origin.

4. What is the derivation of the name badminton?

5. Discuss the unusual shape of the first English courts.

6. Who brought the game to the United States?

7. What is the IBF? When was it first established?

8. Which country won the first international championship?

9. What is the difference between the Thomas Cup and the Uber Cup? How often are these championships held?

10. Name the countries dominating Thomas Cup and Uber Cup play in recent years.

Chapter 2

Equipment and Facilities

Having the proper tools is a prerequisite for success in any endeavor. Badminton is no exception to the rule. Good equipment is a must for all levels of play — from beginner to tournament champion.

Negative feelings toward the sport of badminton have occurred because of inferior and loosely-strung rackets with slick plastic grips, shuttles which fly erratically, sagging nets, poorly kept courts, and windy conditions on outdoor courts. Quality equipment is not unduly expensive when compared to that required of many other sports. When good equipment is purchased initially and properly cared for, it can actually be less expensive than a poorer quality since it will last much longer.

A general rule of thumb for purchasing equipment is to buy the best you can afford and then afford it the best of care. Your instructor can assist you in selecting the best equipment according to your needs. Another suggestion is to experiment with different types of equipment to determine your preference.

The Racket

Although only one racket per participant is used on the court, tournament players usually carry two or more in the event of mishaps. Rackets vary in price from about $6.00 to $60.00 and are constructed of wood, metal, a combination of wood and metal, and various synthetics. Since rules do not specify a legal racket, variations abound. Differences in price are dictated by the material and workmanship. Metal rackets have advantages over wooden rackets in that they can be strung tighter, do not have to be stored to prevent warping, and usually are lighter.

Racket strings are made of nylon and lamb gut. Since gut is more expensive and must be protected from moisture, most players use nylon strings even though gut is more resilient and has more "feel." Good quality nylon is very serviceable, can be strung with high tension, and is resilient to fraying and moisture.

Some of the various types of racquets available

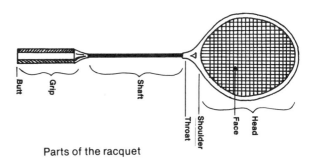

Parts of the racquet

A player's hand size determines the grip size of the racket. These sizes usually vary from 3⅜ to 3⅝ inches. Most adults will use the 3½ inch grip, and the best racket grips are usually made of leather.

Tips for Racket Care

1. Keep wood frame rackets in a press when not in use.
2. Periodically wipe perspiration from hands and racket grip during a match.
3. Inspect racket for damage and repair it quickly.
4. Do not swing rackets at the net, standards or the floor.
5. Doubles partners should ''call'' for shots to avoid collisions.

Shuttlecocks

Shuttlecocks are manufactured from nylon or feathers. The feathered shuttle is made of 14-16 goose feathers inserted in a leather-covered cork base. The feathers in one shuttle are all taken from one wing so they will match and spin correctly during flight. This type shuttle is required for most tournament play and is the legal shuttle described in the rules. Since the feathered shuttle is expensive ($1.20 to $1.40 each) and fragile (seldom lasts a match), it is not used for class instruction or in

many lower level tournaments. A good quality nylon shuttle endures several hours of play, costs approximately 75¢, and exhibits a flight pattern very similar to the feather shuttle. The consistency of the flight pattern of a feathered shuttle has not been duplicated in a nylon shuttle and this is why the feathered shuttle continues to be the choice among experts and tournament officials.

Tips for Care of the Shuttle

1. Always hold the shuttle by the base or lower ribs.
2. Keep feather shuttles in a cool moisturized container when not in use.
3. Store nylon shuttles base down in protective tubes.
4. Keep extra shuttles off the court during play.

Clothing

Official rules do not indicate specific clothing for badminton players. Local custom, club rules, special tournament rules, comfort and common sense in some combination usually dictate what is to be worn. Some clubs still require all white apparel, including warm-ups. From a health and safety point of view, a player should wear a comfortable, loose-fitting shirt and shorts and rubber-soled shoes with a good arch support. To protect the feet from blisters, many players choose to wear two pairs of socks. Some female players wear tennis skirts and dresses. To avoid embarrassment, a player should always check with the tournament director or club pro for possible dress regulations before arriving at the courts.

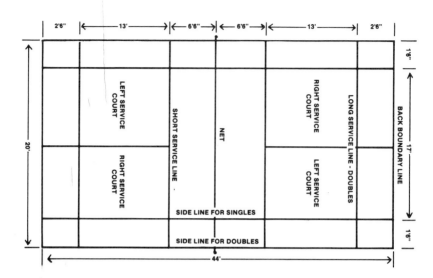

Figure 2-1. The official badminton court

Court and Net

Figure 2-1 illustrates the court specified by the official rules of badminton. Although badminton can be played out-of-doors, all but the most casual beginning level player prefer to play inside, protected from the sun, wind, rain and other distractions. Since most badminton is played in existing gymnasiums, any floor suitable for basketball play is acceptable. The rules specify a 30-foot ceiling for international play but a 25-foot clearance is adequate for other levels of competition.

The net divides the two playing courts and must be stretched between two posts so that it is 5 feet in height at the center, and 5 feet, 1 inch high at the posts. If the posts cannot be placed on the side boundary, this boundary should be marked with a thin post or ribbon attached to the sideline and rising to the net cord.

Tips for Care of Court and Net

1. Keep the floor clean and dry.
2. Carefully fold and store the net in a dry place when not in use.
3. Do not lean or pull on the net or its supports.
4. Carefully remove shuttles that are caught in the net by pushing them through the net from the direction of penetration.

Name_____

Chapter 2 Evaluation

1. What are rackets made of? What are the advantages of the different compositions?

2. What type of stringing for the racket is recommended if economy is a consideration?

3. What is the range of grips available for rackets?

4. List two tips for racket care.

5. Name two advantages for using nylon as opposed to feather shuttles. What is one advantage of the feather shuttle?

6. Describe the clothing requirements for badminton play.

7. Why do serious players prefer indoor badminton?

8. How high should the net be at its corner? At the center?

Chapter 3

Scoring and Playing the Game

Complete badminton rules (or laws, as they are called) are printed in Chapter 18. The present chapter previews simplified rules and procedures to introduce the beginning student to the basic concept of badminton. Terminology and certain "unwritten" rules are also presented later in the chapter. Answers to some of the most often asked questions among beginners follow.

What Is the Game Like?

Badminton is similar to the game of tennis. Singles is played with one player per side, while doubles is played with two players per side. Players propel the shuttle back and forth over a net until an error (fault) is made. Unlike tennis, the projectile (shuttle) is not allowed to bounce.

What Happens First?

Players toss a coin or spin a racket to determine choice of serving or receiving, or court. The winner of the toss makes one choice and the opponent takes the remaining option.

How Is a Game Begun?

One player puts the shuttle in play by striking it underhand across the net to the diagonally opposite court. In singles the shuttle is served and received in the right hand court when the server's score is even (0, 2, 4, 6, etc.), and in the left court when the score is odd (1, 3, 5, etc.). This procedure requires that both receiver and server change service courts after a point is made. In doubles the partner in the right hand court begins the inning of service for the team by serving to the opponent who is in his/her right hand court. If a point is scored, the server changes service courts and serves to the other opponent. If the serving team fails to win the rally, the server's partner then serves unless it is the beginning service of the game. The team which serves first in each game is allowed only one partner's service.

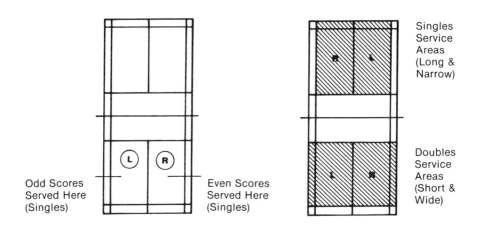

Singles Service Areas (Long & Narrow)

Doubles Service Areas (Short & Wide)

Odd Scores Served Here (Singles)

Even Scores Served Here (Singles)

How Long Is a Game?

Women's singles games consist of 11 points. Men's singles and all doubles games consist of 15 points.

Does Badminton Have a Score Like the "Deuce" in Tennis?

Yes, when an 11 point game is tied at 9-all, the player who reached 9 points first has the option of "setting the game" for 3 additional points. If tied at 10-all the game may be set for 2 additional points. In the 15 point games, the setting option for a tie of 13-all is 5 points and for a tie of 14-all, 3 points. If the side that reached the tie score first chooses to set, the score is called 0-0 (love-all) and the side that reaches the set score first is the winner of the game. If the appropriate team does not choose to set, the regular game score (11 or 15) is used as the end of the game.

How Are Points Scored?

When faults are committed by the receiving side, points are scored by the serving side. When the serving side commits a fault, no points are scored and another server takes over.

What Are Common Faults?

It is a fault (1) to hit the shuttle twice in succession or carry it on the racket momentarily during a rally; (2) to reach over the net to hit the shuttle or allow the shuttle to hit the body or clothing of a player; (3) to touch the net or its supports with racket, body, or clothing; or (4) to cause the shuttle to fall outside the appropriate boundary lines.

What Is a Match?

Winning two out of three games is an official match.

Who Keeps Score?

Players generally do their own scoring and officiating unless they are participating in high level tournaments. Players are responsible for making line calls on their sides of the net and calling their own faults. The server should announce the score before each service in order to avoid misunderstandings. The server's score is always called first.

Points of Player Etiquette

1. Introduce yourself to your partner and opponents if necessary. Shake hands with opponents and partner after a match.
2. Bring two or three new shuttles for club or tournament play unless other provisions are made.
3. Warm up your opponent by hitting strokes that can be returned; do not "kill" every stroke.
4. Control your emotions and temper at all times.
5. Return the shuttle to the server after each point.
6. Avoid talk and other distractions while your opponent is serving or returning the shuttle.
7. Call fault decisions immediately and do not question your opponent's decisions. Give opponents the benefit of the doubt on close calls.
8. Avoid making excuses for poor shots.
9. Show consideration for players on other courts. Never cross an occupied court except during a break in play.
10. Compliment your opponent's good shots.
11. Never give unsolicited advice to partner or opponent.
12. Avoid abuse of shuttle, net, racket or court.
13. Offer to replay a point if there was interference.
14. Keep play continuous.
15. In tournament play, immediately report all scores to the tournament director.

Shaking hands with your partner and opponents after a match is good player etiquette.

TERMINOLOGY

ALLEY: The extended area on both sides of the court used in doubles play and the area in the back of the court between rear boundary and along service lines.

BACKCOURT: The rear half of the court.

BALK: A preliminary feint before a stroke; illegal in badminton.

BIRD: Common terminology for shuttlecock or shuttle.

BLOCK: To cause the shuttlecock to rebound off the racket into the opponent's court without swinging at the bird.

CARRY: Allowing the shuttlecock to rest momentarily on the racket during a stroke. An illegal procedure.

CLEAR: A shot hit with a high trajectory which lands in the back court.

COMBINATION DOUBLES FORMATION: A method of play in doubles where partners rotate from up-and-back to side-by-side as the circumstances dictate.

COURT: The area where the game is played (20 × 44 feet for doubles, and 17 × 44 feet for singles).

DRIVE: A shot hit with a flat trajectory — nearly parallel to the floor.

DRIVE SERVE: A sharply hit serve with a flat trajectory.

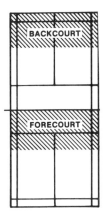

DROP: A softly hit shot that barely clears the net and lands in the forecourt.

FAULT: Any violation of the rules.

FOOT FAULT: Violation of the rules involving the server or receiver being in an illegal position during the serve.

FORECOURT: The front half of the court near the net.

FLICK SERVE: A deceptive serve hit quickly with forearm rotation in an attempt to pass the receiver who is rushing the net.

GAME: A unit of scoring, 15 points in men's singles and all doubles, and 11 points in women's singles.

HAND-IN: Player serving retains the serve.

HAND-OUT: Used in doubles to denote one partner has lost service.

IBF: International Badminton Federation, an organization to promote and sponsor international tournaments.

INNING: The time period when a side or individual holds service.

"IN" SIDE: Player or team who is serving.

LET: A legal stoppage of play which allows a replay of the point in progress at that time.

LOVE: A score of zero or nothing. Love-all (0-0) is used to begin a game.

MATCH: A unit of scoring made up of games, usually the best two of three games.

MIXED DOUBLES: A team composed of one male and one female.

NET SHOT: A shot made from the forecourt that trickles over the net.

"OUT" SIDE: The team or individual who is not serving.

OVERHEAD: A shot hit above the head.

POINT: The smallest unit of scoring.

PRONATION: Inward movement of the wrist and forearm which provides the power for the forehand strokes.

RACKET: Implement used for striking the shuttlecock.

RALLY: To hit the shuttlecock back and forth between opponents.

READY POSITION: Body position allowing quick movement in any direction.

RECEIVER: Player to whom the service is directed.

ROUND THE HEAD SHOT: A shot hit with forehand technique on the backhand side of the body.

SERVE: The act of placing the shuttlecock in play.

SERVER: The player who delivers the service.

SERVICE COURT: Designated area of the court into which the serve must be delivered.

SETTING: Method of lengthening the game to play off ties. The player who is tied has the option of extending.

SHORT SERVICE LINE: The line on the court that serves must cross to be legal. The line is located $6\frac{1}{2}$ feet from the net.

SHUTTLECOCK: The object that is hit by the racket; commonly called the shuttle or the bird.

SIDE-BY-SIDE: Method of playing doubles when partners stay adjacent to one another.

SMASH: A hard hit shot with a steep downward trajectory.

SUPINATION: Opposite movement to pronation, used for backhand shots for power.

USBA: United States Badminton Association, regulates and promotes badminton in the United States.

UP AND BACK: A method of doubles play when one partner plays forecourt and the other plays backcourt.

WOOD SHOT: A shot causing the shuttle to contact the frame of the racket. Currently a legal shot.

Chapter 4

Gripping the Racket

While strokes, footwork, and speed are all necessary ingredients to good badminton, nothing is more important than starting with the correct grip.

Because an improper grip restricts arm movement, thus causing undue muscle fatigue and decreased stroke effectiveness, it can truly be said that a proper grip is the foundation of good badminton play.

Three grips may be used in playing badminton: forehand, backhand, and frying pan. Some players find they can be effective using only one grip — the forehand; however, most players find the use of the backhand grip adds more power to their strokes.

Forehand

This "Universal" grip is similar to the Eastern forehand grip in tennis with the V formed by the thumb and index finger on the top bevel of the racket grip. One way to assume the "Universal" grip is described below.

1. Hold the racket by its throat in your nondominant hand so that the racket head is perpendicular to the floor and the racket extends lengthwise away from you with the handle pointing toward you. (See Figure 4-1.)
2. Reaching forward with your dominant hand, "shake hands" with the racket using a light grip with your fingers and thumb. (See Figure 4-2.)
3. Check to see if there is a V on top formed by thumb and index finger.
4. Check the underside of the grip to see if the fingers are spread with extra space between index and middle finger forming a "trigger finger." (See Figure 4-3.)
5. Check the end of the racket to be sure the butt of the racket presses into the heel of the hand.

Ready position showing forehand grip

Figure 4-1. Hold racquet by the throat, with racquet head perpendicular to the floor.

Figure 4-2. "Shake hands" with the racquet.

Figure 4-3. A "trigger finger" forms on the underside of the grip.

Figure 4-4. For more power on backhand strokes, the thumb is changed to a straighter position.

This grip should help you to feel that the racket is an extension of your arm and hand. With your palm and racket face facing in the same direction, the thumb and first two fingers will supply the majority of the gripping power so they should exert more pressure on the grip than the last two fingers. No pressure should be felt in the palm or at the junction between thumb and index finger since the racket is held by the fingers. The total feel of the grip should be of firmness when the shuttle is contacted and relaxation between strokes. A tight rigid grip with bunched fingers is to be avoided.

Backhand

For the backhand grip, the position of the thumb is changed from being wrapped around the handle to a straighter position on the side of the handle away from the hitting surface (See Figure 4-4). This allows the thumb to push the racket through the air and provides greater force and speed.

Frying Pan

The "frying pan" or "hammer" grip is used in doubles play by some players for serving, return of service, and net play. This grip is assumed by laying the racket flat on the floor and reaching down and picking it up with the V of thumb and index finger on the upward side of the racket grip. (See Figure 4-5.) The racket face will be perpendicular to the palm and parallel with the net. The racket should be held near the top of the leather grip in a "choked-up" manner (See Figure 4-6). The head of the racket is always pointed up. The advantage of this grip under these circumstances is control.

Figure 4-5. The frying pan grip is assumed by laying the racquet flat on the floor and picking it up with the V on the upward side.

Figure 4-6. The racket is held near the top of the grip in a choked-up manner, with the head of the racquet pointed up.

Name_____

Chapter 4 Evaluation

1. Why is a good grip so important for a badminton player? List two problems that can be caused by a poor grip.

2. Describe the procedure for assuming the proper grip, and list the three checkpoints.

3. How do players compensate for lack of strength for backhand strokes?

4. Describe the "frying pan" or "hammer" grip. When is it used?

Chapter 5

Principles of Stroking

A principle is a guideline with a broad application for action. This chapter presents certain principles to assist you in playing a better game of badminton. However, there are exceptions to all rules, and the chapters on specific skills should be consulted for special applications.

Mental Principles

Some of the more important mental principles of badminton often apply to other games as well. They are:

CONCENTRATION — Keep your mind alert, know where your opponent is at all times, and make each shot your best effort. Try to watch the shuttle until it makes contact with your racket.

ANTICIPATION — Out-think your opponent by planning ahead, scout your opponent to discover his/her weaknesses and tendencies, and be ready for the unexpected also.

FLEXIBILITY — Change your tactics when losing. Adjust your play to counteract your opponent's strategy.

EXPLOITATION — Use your best strokes; avoid your weaknesses. If you are in better physical condition than your opponent, use it to your advantage.

DECEPTION — Make all stroke preparations (backswing, stance, etc.) as similar as possible so the opponent will not be able to anticipate your shot.

Mechanical Principles

The mechanical principles related to badminton help players understand why certain movement and techniques are necessary and motivate a closer attendance to detail in stroking.

POWER PRODUCTION — The amount of power transferred from racket to shuttle at the point of contact is directly related to the speed of the racket at impact. Deep clears, deep serves, drives and smashes utilize a near-maximum amount of speed.

As more body parts are involved, more force can be generated. Body muscle force must be applied in a sequential order to be effective. The basic sequence is weight shift, hip rotation, shoulder rotation, arm extension and forearm rotation. Students should attempt to use the full sequence of movement, when maximum speed of racket head is desired.

Momentum is developed through distance and by time. Theoretically, the more distance and time in which the racket has to travel before contact point, the faster it should be moving at that point. This concept emphasizes the need for a long backswing in preparation for a stroke. The racket head is dropped behind the back in a good backswing.

For the long backswing which results in increased speed, drop the racquet head behind the back.

A short lever produces maximum rotary speed. The motion of the arm during stroking is an arc, part of a circle. If the whole arm were extended during the rotation, the movement would be slower than it is when the elbow is bent. This fast movement allows the racket to build momentum. The elbow should remain in a flexed position during the backswing and forward movement so that maximum speed can occur.

The elbow should remain flexed during the backswing and foreward movement.

An extended arm at contact transfers speed.

A long lever produces maximum linear speed. The shuttle travels in a line, linear motion. In order to generate the maximum speed at the point of contact between racket and shuttle, the arm should be extended. This will transfer the greatest speed available.

The effectiveness of a force produced by the body is dependent upon the interaction of body and racket. Since the grip connects the speed of force of the body to the racket, it **must be firm** to transfer the full amount of speed available.

CONTROL — The companion to power is control. Access to all the power in the world is ineffective if it is not channelled properly. The shuttle must travel where you want it to go to be effective and must land within the boundaries to be legal.

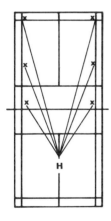

Control means hitting where you aim.

The longer the shuttle is in contact with the racket, the greater the control. The shuttle will assume the same pathway and speed as the racket. Therefore, a player should swing through the shuttle and finish with **a good follow-through.** This is important for softly hit shots, like the drops, as well as harder hit shots.

The angle of the racket face at contact determines direction. The shuttle takes a path that is perpendicular to the face of the racket. If a shot is meant to travel upward, the racket face should be tilted toward the ceiling (open face). If meant to travel downward, a racket tilted toward the floor is necessary (closed face). If a flight parallel to the floor is desired, the racket must be in a right angle position to the floor (square or flat face). Shuttle position relative to the body of the player facilitates hitting with the desired angle. It is easier to hit with

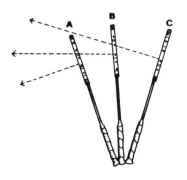

RACQUET FACE ANGLES:
A = closed; B = square; C = open

a downward angle if the shuttle is out in front of the body and easier to hit upward if the shuttle is directly overhead.

Speed of the racket determines distance traveled, not direction. By varying the speed of the racket, many strokes are executed with the same technique. An overhead drop is merely an overhead clear executed slowly. It travels in the same basic pathway but, due to less speed, begins to be affected by air resistance more quickly and rapidly drops to the court.

Name_____

Chapter 5 Evaluation

1. List four guidelines for winning the mental game of badminton.

2. What is the purpose of learning physical principles related to badminton?

3. Describe the sequential action of the body in producing the maximum speed for swinging a racket.

4. What principle explains the need for a long backswing in producing the high speed racket swing?

5. Why should the elbow remain flexed throughout the major portion of the stroke?

6. Linear speed is greater when a lever is what length?

(Over)

7. Explain the need for a lengthy follow-through from a mechanical point of view.

8. If a shuttle is hit with a racket in a closed face position, which direction will it travel?

9. If you want to hit a shuttle downard as in a smash, where should the shuttle be in relation to your body when you strike it?

10. What is the major factor that determines whether a shuttle that is hit overhead will be a drop shot or a deep clear?

Chapter 6

Footwork

Footwork is the procedure used to move from place to place on the badminton court. The stroke cannot be effective if the player is not in position to contact the shuttle correctly. Footwork will be efficient and purposeful if the player arrives at the appropriate spot on the court before the shuttle does, if the body is in the correct alignment for the selected stroke, and if the body weight is on the correct foot. Also, good footwork makes it possible to recover efficiently after a stroke and to return to a ready position for the next stroke. Any pattern of movement that fulfills these requirements would be correct (adequate) and past experience with sports and personal preference play a part in determining footwork patterns.

This chapter will present suggestions of acceptable footwork for the beginning player to use while establishing a personal movement pattern that works best for him/her. **Note:** Footwork movements listed in this chapter are for right-handed players. Left-handed players should reverse the procedures.

The following guidelines will help establish good footwork patterns:

1. Return to home position after every stroke. If there is not enough time, recover as much as you can but maintain a stationary position while your opponent strokes the shuttle. It is easier to begin to move from a stationary position than to change direction while moving.

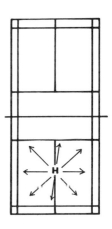

Areas to cover from home position

31

2. Keep your eye on the shuttle at all times.

3. Begin the backswing of the racket while moving into position. This will allow a faster response.

4. Try to take fewer steps by stretching and lunging to hit the shuttle. This facilitates a quick recovery.

READY POSITION

Ready Position

While waiting for an opponent to stroke the bird, a player should assume a stationary position that will allow quick movement in any direction. The feet should be placed in a side stride position about shoulder-width apart. Keep body weight evenly distributed over both feet and balanced front to back. The knees should be bent slightly. The racket should be held with the head up and slightly toward the backhand side of the body.

A player's ready position should be a position from which he/she can readily move to all other areas of the court. While receiving a serve, this "home base" position is approximately halfway between the short service line and the rear line of the service court. Right-handed players stand near the center line in the right service court and 3 to 4 feet away from the center line in the left court. Left-handed players take the opposite positions. This arrangement permits the majority of returns to be made with the forehand. Some players stand with the left foot ahead of the right foot to facilitate movement in up and back directions. After the service, the player takes a home base position about 2 to 3 feet back of the middle of the court with feet on either side of the middle line.

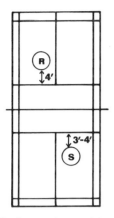

Singles service positions

Serving position

Movement to Sidelines

To move to the forehand side, pivot on the left foot and take steps with alternate feet ending with weight on the left foot, which will be nearer the sideline than the other foot. Move to the backhand side by pivoting on the right foot and taking alternating steps to the sideline ending with weight on the right foot.

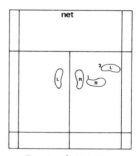

Forehand Sideline

Movement to the Upper Corners

To move to the diagonal upper corner of the court for a forehand, push off with the left foot and take alternating steps in a diagonal pathway ending on the left foot. For a backhand upper corner shot, push off with the right foot and take steps with alternating feet. The last step is taken with the right foot.

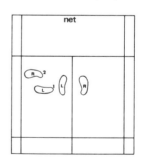

Backhand Sideline

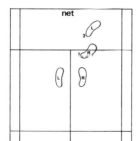

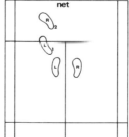

Upper Forehand Corner   Upper Backhand Corner

Movement to the Rear Corners

Movement to the forehand rear corner can be executed by using running steps or by using sliding or shuffle steps. The running steps are faster; the sliding steps keep the body in a better hitting posture and provide better vision. The running method involves a reverse pivot on the left foot and diagonal steps toward the rear corner ending with the weight on the right foot. The sliding method begins with a quarter-turn backward pivot with the left foot, a sideward step with the other foot, and a closing step with the left foot beside the right foot.

This pattern of step and close is repeated and a last step is taken with the right foot. A player should experiment with each method to determine the most effective and efficient way to move.

Movement to the backhand rear corner uses a reverse pivot on the right foot and running steps ending on the left foot. Keep the shuttle in view while running by looking over the right shoulder.

Note: Illustrations are for right-handed players.

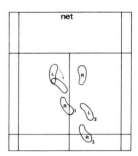

Rear Forehand Corner
Running Style

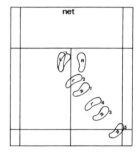

Rear Forehand Corner
Sliding Style

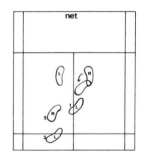

Rear Backhand Corner

Name_____

Chapter 6 Evaluation

1. What are the purposes of good footwork?

2. Explain the five guides to good footwork.

3. Describe the ready position.

4. Where is the home base for receiving serves? For normal play?

5. Describe footwork patterns for the corners of the court.

Chapter 7

The Forehand

Since the various styles of gripping the racket have been covered in Chapter 4, it is now time to proceed with the fundamentals of the forehand stroke. Because this stroke is without doubt the most popular stroke in the game of badminton, we will cover it thoroughly.

As you prepare for your opponent's stroke, remember that you must assume a "ready position." The ready position places you on your toes with your weight equally distributed on both feet, ready to move and react instantly in the direction of the shuttle.

The racket is held high, with a forehand grip, as you anticipate the direction of your opponent's shot.

In singles, your position should be about four feet behind the short service line and centered in the court. The doubles position, when anticipating the serve, will place you in the center of the doubles court on your side, with equal coverage to all corners of the receiving area.

For a right-handed player, the forehand stroke is made when receiving a shuttle to the right side. The reverse is true for the left-handed player. Thus, as the shuttle is struck by the opponent, assume a position so that the shuttle and your body are in the best position to make the stroke as successful as possible.

As the shuttle approaches, quickly shift your position so that your left side is to the net, keeping the shuttle in front of you whenever possible. At times you will need very little movement in order to stroke the shuttle; on the other hand, there are times when you are only a step away. Then again, there are times when you must quickly step and stretch to reach the shuttle. Review the previous chapter on footwork to understand how the stroke and the position of the feet blend together to achieve maximum results.

Ready position for receiving in singles

Ready positions for receiving in doubles

As you position yourself for the incoming shuttle, begin to prepare the racket for the forehand stroke. Quickly take the racket behind your back in a bent arm motion, just as though you were taking a flyswatter back to swing at a fly. At this point, you must tighten your grip on the handle of the racket, for the stroke will be a forceful one, and you must maintain control of the racket and not have it leave your hand. Cock your wrist, but be sure that you are relaxed and comfortable in your arm position.

As you begin your forward stroke, whip the racket into the shuttle, stroking it with a flat racket face, utilizing the wrist to aid in propelling the racket head into the shuttle. Remember that the net is five feet high at the lowest point; therefore, in order to clear the net, it is necessary to stroke the shuttle with a "low to high" racket swing. However, be careful not to lift the shuttle so high that you offer a set-up for your opponent, or one that will carry out of bounds.

We cannot overemphasize the importance of flexibility of the wrist in accelerating the head of the racket. This flexibility, combined with the leverage of the arm, allows a definite "whip" action, which is constantly utilized in stroking the shuttle.

If the shuttle is flying at a trajectory that does not require a low to high stroke, then you may obtain an attack sequence by driving the shuttle downwards into your opponent's court.

The follow-through must be complete, relaxed, and fully **under control**, due to the necessity for a rapid recovery.

You are literally "on your toes" at this time, and moving quickly to resume proper court position for adequate coverage for the return shot.

FOREHAND STROKE

Closeup of wrist position in forehand

Low trajectory forehand

Try to shift your weight into the shuttle when you strike it — the shuttle will be propelled deep into the backcourt.

Most experienced players will quickly realize the desirability of propelling the shuttle deep in the opponent's court. Sometimes this is difficult because of improper technique, the lightness of the shuttle, or a player's lack of strength. To assist you in achieving this difficult task to a high degree of regularity, you must attempt to **shift your weight** into the shuttle when you stroke it. In doing this, you will find that success is easier to achieve when you prepare early. It costs nothing and produces good results.

As previously stated, it is desirable to contact the shuttle in front of the body. This contact area is a comfortable reach to the right front side of the body, about two feet to the right side of the left, or forward foot. This enables you to place the drive with sufficient force in any direction you might choose.

Remember, this is the **fastest** net game in the world, so be prepared to move quickly and to change directions with lightning speed. Also, watching your opponents closely will often dictate where they plan to hit it, so be alert.

One valuable suggestion that you should always remember is to **keep your eye on the shuttle at all times**.

Tips on Technique in the Forehand

1. Anticipate your opponent's next shot and be prepared to move rapidly.
2. Maintain a loose forehand grip, and support the racket by both hands as you await your opponent's stroke.
3. Always think one stroke ahead of the opponent, and mentally prepare to stroke the shuttle to that area left open.
4. Return back to your home position quickly after each stroke.
5. Be on your toes with your weight equally distributed.
6. Take your racket back early in preparation for the stroke.
7. Vary the direction of your return shot; keep the opponent guessing.
8. Watch the shuttle into the strings of your racket.

Name_____

Chapter 7 Evaluation

1. What is the predominant grip for the forehand stroke?

2. Explain the use of wrist action in executing the forehand.

3. How can you develop deception when using the forehand?

4. Why is the transfer of weight helpful? When should the transfer be made?

5. Define your position in singles with relationship to the strategy you are planning to use in the game.

6. Why is it necessary to bring the racket behind the back during the backswing phase of the stroke?

7. What is the "low-to-high" procedure in stroking? What does this have to do with strategy?

8. Why is it desirable to stroke the shuttle deep into the backcourt on forehand returns?

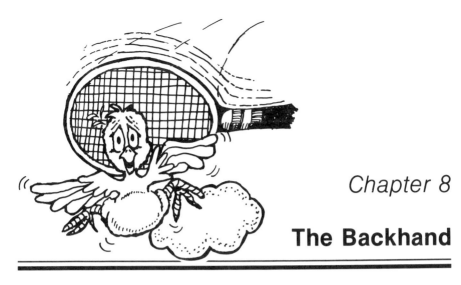

Chapter 8

The Backhand

As is the case in most racket sports, the forehand is the "bread and butter" stroke, and the backhand is somewhat weaker. This is usually due to insufficient understanding and practice of the techniques of the various backhand shots one might be called upon to execute during a game. In this chapter, we shall thoroughly cover the backhand to give you a comprehensive picture of the stroke.

Any intelligent player can quickly determine if an opponent has a weak backhand. Most will see this in the warm-up phase of the contest. Smart players look for weaknesses in their opponents, and this one is hard to hide.

To change to the backhand grip, turn the racket handle one-quarter turn and place the thumb on the back side of the handle. The thumb print is located squarely on the flat portion of the back of the grip. You will quickly see the necessity for this when you begin to use the stroke.

As the shuttle is hit by the opponent, and you see it heading toward the backhand, immediately adjust your footwork and turn your right side toward the net. As you make this footwork change, shift the racket handle into the backhand grip. A little practice will make this easy to accomplish, and after a few times this change will not seem uncomfortable for you.

Place your weight on your rear foot, and prepare to meet the incoming shuttle. As you take your racket back into the backswing position, you will notice that the elbow bends comfortably, and the racket head flows in close to your left side. The right elbow is "pointing at the shuttle," so to speak. Be sure to cock the wrist as you proceed into the backswing portion of the stroke, as this motion will greatly aid you in achieving depth on your backhand.

It is your intention to stroke the shuttle at a point about two to three feet to the side of the body, with the total effort of your stroke going into the hit. At

THE BACKHAND

The Backhand Grip: **Top,** front view; **Bottom,** rear view

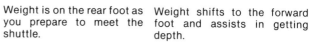

Weight is on the rear foot as you prepare to meet the shuttle.

Weight shifts to the forward foot and assists in getting depth.

THE BACKHAND SEQUENCE

the precise moment, swing the racket head into the path of the shuttle, whipping the wrist and also the elbow into your stroke. Continue to lead the stroke with your racket head to assure a quality stroke and a proper follow-through. Although you are guiding the racket head into the shuttle, you are, in a sense, "throwing" the racket into the shuttle.

Remember to watch the shuttle at all times, even trying to see it onto the strings of the racket.

Be sure to recover quickly to your "home" position, centering yourself into a position to cover sufficiently all areas of the court with equal ease.

A very critical factor for success on the backhand side will be to **keep the shuttle in front of you.** That is to say, don't let it get behind you. Your contact point should be in front of the forward (right) shoulder. A proper weight shift will also greatly assist in getting additional depth on the backhand. Remember, this is a difficult stroke, and it will be played extensively by your opponent to capitalize on your weakness, if any.

Remember the old saying, "Practice makes perfect." It holds true here, so give yourself plenty of time to work on this stroke, and you will be confident when you begin to compete.

Tips on Techniques for the Backhand

1. Observe your opponent during the warm-up to determine if he or she has a weak backhand.
2. Practice changing grips frequently, until you can do it automatically. Practice will eliminate the need to use two hands as you change the grip.
3. Turn your side promptly and begin your backswing early.
4. Remember to point the elbow toward the shuttle.
5. Lay the wrist back early, and use it in the stroke to give additional depth.
6. Whip the head of the racket into the shuttle, grasping the handle firmly.
7. Be sure to keep the shuttle in front of your body.
8. When possible, step into the stroke, as this will provide you with additional power in your shot.
9. Recover quickly to your home position, ready for the next shot.

Name_____

Chapter 8 Evaluation

1. Why is it desirable to contact the shuttle in front of the body?

2. Explain the change of grip from the forehand to the backhand.

3. The opponent will look for a definite weakness in this stroke. Why?

4. What is the purpose of having the thumb flat against the side of the racket handle when changing from forehand to backhand?

5. How will the shift of weight aid you in achieving depth?

6. What purpose does the elbow play in stroking the shuttle with the backhand stroke?

7. The combination of thumb, wrist and elbow, with shoulder turn, are all important in the backhand stroke. Why?

8. What are the limitations of using the forehand grip on the backhand side?

Chapter 9

The Service

The service is the stroke used to initiate play. It is used to begin each point in the match. The service is an underhand stroke and is described that way within the rules of the game. It begins as a defensive play, in that you must strike the shuttle below the waist and hit it upward over the net. This makes it a defensive stroke.

The service is a very important shot, for if it is executed poorly, the opponent will immediately take advantage of the situation and either win the point instantly, or hit a counter shot that immediately puts the server at a strong disadvantage. Therefore, placement of the shuttle, and in-depth knowledge of game strategy and serving, are extremely important to the beginning and intermediate player.

Deception is important in serving. It is well within the scope of the game to anticipate accurately the type of service the opponent will execute and thus have an excellent head start toward returning the shuttle and taking the offense.

Accurate placement of the service can win a point outright, or it can put the opponent at such a disadvantage that he/she cannot gain the attack, thus opening up the court for the server. Therefore, one must continually practice this important skill in order to perfect it.

As you note your opponent's position, you will do well to notice the obvious parts of the receiving court that are not covered. It is to these areas that you must direct your serve, keeping in mind that your opponent is hoping you will serve a "set-up" serve that can be readily smashed at you or can open part of your court.

Serves in badminton are basically one of two kinds, either **short and low,** or **high and deep.** The short and low serve is used mainly in doubles due to the shortness of the length of the service court, and also due to the fact that the service court is a foot and a half wider, allowing more space to hit.

SERVICE
STANCE

Wrist cocked
for service

Position of the Server

In singles the server stands with both feet well within the serving court, as specified in the rules. Remember that a part of both feet must remain in contact with the court at the moment of contact. Your basic position will be three to four feet behind the short service line, and about two feet from the center line. Since your service is always at a diagonal, you must target the part of the receiver's court most open to you. This will usually be the deep backhand corner of the receiving court.

Target area for doubles service (usually short and low)

Target area for singles (high deep serve)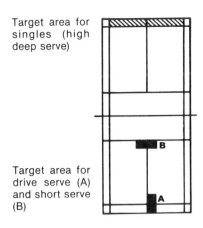

Target area for drive serve (A) and short serve (B)

In doubles your opponent will not have to retrieve your service from the depth allowed in singles, due to the long service line being two feet six inches closer. Thus, the short service is more popular and is used most of the time. In order to have the best advantage in serving the short serve, the server moves forward slightly from the singles service position, closer to the short service line, almost "in the corner" of the service court. Remember that your opponent will be expecting the short service, so master the fundamentals and practice regularly so that you can achieve good results with your service and still maintain the element of surprise in your strategy.

One strategy used by skilled players is to disguise the type of serve they plan to use. In doing this, the player simply lays the wrist back when stroking either the short or long service. Only the server knows the type of service to be used, so the receiver is on the defense. If the short service is used, the wrist remains laid back throughout the stroke. If the server desires to use the long deep serve, the wrist is brought into play at the last moment, sending the shuttle deep over the head of the intended receiver. Give it a try; it works! You may certainly use this motion no matter which service position you are using, since one produces a short, shallow serve and the other, a deep high serve.

Stance

Your footwork placement during the service attempt is called your stance. The stance is designed to place you in the best position to maximize your effectiveness in serving. As you assume this position on the court, carefully prepare yourself for the service procedure. Remember to take your time.

Assume a position with your left foot in front of the right, with the feet spread a comfortable distance apart. The forward foot should be pointed in the general direction of the receiving court. The knees are flexed comfortably and the weight is distributed evenly, allowing the weight to flow from the rear foot to the forward foot into the stroke.

The rear foot, when in the service position, is at an angle to the forward foot. This provides greater comfort when it is necessary to move toward the shuttle after the service has been made. This angle is to the right sideline of the court. Practice this a few times and it will feel very comfortable for you.

Footwork stance for serve

Grips

The basic grip for serving is the Eastern forehand (or "Universal") grip described in Chapter 2. This is the most comfortable and most versatile of the grips used in the game. You will return to it most requently when you are in a waiting position. It is the grip used most for the service, as it best accentuates the laid-back wrist theory.

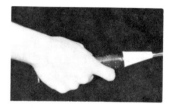

The basic forehand grip for serving

The "frying pan" grip is sometimes used in serving the short service for doubles and in returning doubles serves with net shots. It utilizes a shortened grip which the user will find detrimental to the deep game. The learner should experiment with each type of grip to determine which is preferable, and then learn to use it well. Be award, however, of the limitations of the "frying pan" grip.

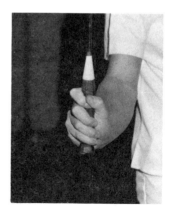

The "frying pan" grip

Holding the Shuttle

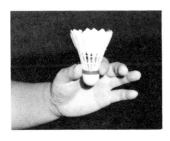

Holding the shuttle by the base

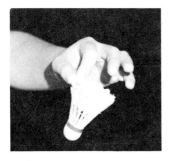

Holding the shuttle by the feathers

Whether the shuttle is made of nylon or feathers, care should be taken in its use and handling during the game. Although holding the shuttle for the service is almost an automatic procedure, we shall briefly explain the method.

Grasp the shuttle by the base (cork) with the thumb and forefinger of the left hand as you prepare to serve. This gives stability to the shuttle and helps to assure a secure stroke.

There are players who hold the shuttle by the nylon skirt or by the feathers, but they are few in number. While this procedure is not harmful to the shuttle, it is not as secure as you prepare to stroke the service.

Since disguise is a part of the service, you should learn to hold the shuttle the same way for all types of serves. This way, you will not telegraph your intentions to your opponent. Many opponents will look for signs that give away your strategy, so be alert to this as you develop your service motion.

Once you have positioned yourself properly for the service, prepare to serve the shuttle by holding it (as described above) by the thumb and forefinger, and extend the shuttle away from the body an arm's length, in a comfortable position. The elbow should be slightly flexed and not straight. The arm should be relaxed at all times.

As you begin the service motion, the arm holding the shuttle is at a position almost shoulder high; the shuttle is dropped from this position and contact is made with the racket slightly below the waist.

A short serve en-
croachment

Sizing Up the Opponent

Once you have taken your stance, and are preparing to serve, be sure to **take your time.** There is no hurry, and concentration is now very important. Look for telltale signs that show the intentions of your opponent: Will the opponent charge the serve? Drop back as soon as the shuttle is hit? Stay his/her ground?

In an effort to cover the short serve, the opponent will sometimes encroach toward the net at the instant the shuttle is struck on the service. The alert server, sensing this, can immediately win the point with the flick of the wrist, initiating either the flick (drive) serve or the high deep serve. This does take practice, and good anticipation on your part, but continued practice makes it happen.

If the opponent has trouble returning deep serves, then use this serve. Remember that the deep serve, properly placed, does not allow the receiver to make contact until he or she moves deep to the rear of the court. The trajectory of the deep serve is almost vertical in the back, and returns from this position are very difficult — often times setting up the server for the immediate kill shot.

TYPES OF SERVES

Basically, three types of serves are used in badminton:

1. The high deep serve (singles)
2. The short serve (doubles)
3. The drive serve (singles or doubles)

Let us look closely at these serves to better understand the advantages and disadvantages of each.

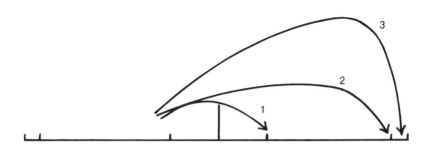

Diagram illustrating the three types of serves: 1 = short serve; 2 = drive serve; 3 = deep serve.

The High Deep Serve

This serve is the basis for the attack in singles, where the service court is narrow but deep. This serve carries to the back line of the court, thus making a return from that area difficult. If the serve is deep and also to the backhand, the return is even more troublesome.

The stance for all serves is the same, but the position will vary for the server depending on whether singles or doubles is being played.

As the stance is assumed, the server carefully observes the position of the receiver. Holding the shuttle by the cork base, and maintaining the forehand grip on the handle of the racket, the server establishes a position with the racket in the backswing motion, pointing to the rear of the server. The shuttle is held at shoulder length in a comfortable position. The server should cock the wrist at this point.

Without moving the feet, shift the weight to the rear foot. As the weight is moved forward, bring the racket down in a sweeping motion. This underhand motion should be timed to contact the shuttle in front of the body, between the knee and the waist. Just prior to contact, bring the wrist into play by flexing it into the stroke. This wrist movement will increase the head speed of the racket sufficiently to give you the depth and heighth your service needs to be effective.

Be sure to hit through the shuttle and continue your swing upward to finish high above the head with your racket. Practice will help you appreciate the importance of combined height and depth. Placement to both the forehand and backhand area of the receiver's court enables you to establish various attack patterns as part of your match strategy.

The Short Serve

Obtain the same stance described earlier for the doubles service. As you move the racket into the backswing position, lay the wrist back and prepare to drop the shuttle for the service. Bring the racket forward into the shuttle, contacting it in front of the body. At the moment of contact, keep the wrist in the laid-back position without moving it. You are now stroking the shuttle with only an arm movement. This assures the low trajector you must have to serve properly in doubles. Considerable practice is needed to instill confidence in the doubles serve, since your opponent is immediately in front of you and ready to pounce on the slightest error.

The Drive Serve

This serve is a combination of the other two, and is used both in singles and doubles to catch the opponent off guard. It is not used as a regular serve, but as an infrequent one. The trajectory is unlike the short serve and the high deep serve. The driven serve has a long, low, flat trajectory, angling quickly toward the backcourt. The server usually contacts the shuttle with a flat racket swing, thus eliminating the higher trajectory. The wrist is brought into play to accelerate the speed of the shuttle past the receiver. When used with discretion, this serve is an effective point maker, and is one that should be practiced often to develop expertise.

Tips on Techniques for Serving

1. Practice the serve often to achieve confidence in mounting the attack.
2. Relax when preparing to serve. This will allow you to move more comfortably and execute more accurately.
3. Concentrate on your position and on your opponent. Try to anticipate his/her moves and strategy.
4. Establish your own game plan, beginning with the proper serve.
5. Stroke the shuttle with confidence.
6. Practice the laid-back wrist effect until it becomes automatic.
7. Shift the weight into the shuttle, especially when using the long deep serve, to give yourself the depth you need to mount the attack.
8. Aim high and deep in singles; aim low and short in doubles.
9. Drop the shuttle just prior to making the forward swing with the racket.
10. Onoo you strike the shuttle, recover quickly to prepare for the return.

Name_____

Chapter 9 Evaluation

1. Briefly describe the singles and doubles serves with regard to strategy.

2. How does the wrist come into play in the driven serve?

3. The rules of serving are very specific. Explain them.

4. How does the service court differ in singles and doubles?

5. Why is the short service used primarily in doubles, and the high deep serve in singles?

6. Generally, where is the best place to aim the high deep service? Why?

(Over)

7. How does your service position change from singles to doubles?

8. Explain the lay back of the wrist in the doubles serve. When would you use it and in what manner?

9. Why is serving a defensive stroke?

10. Is the receiver more apt to charge the net in singles or doubles? Explain this strategy.

Chapter 10
Net Play

Once you have achieved a measure of success in developing the forehand, backhand and service, it is time to broaden your skills through various forms of net play. By using drop shots, you will soon discover new dimensions that add considerable strategy and finesse to the game of badminton.

There are four basic types of drop shots: (1) the hairpin drop; (2) the cross-court drop; (3) the overhead drop; and (4) the underhand drop. Each drop shot is unique in that it possesses the elements of surprise which often catch the opponent guessing about your strategy. Once these strokes are learned, you will want to disguise them to add more difficulties for your opponent.

The Hairpin Drop

The basic flight of the hairpin drop shot is just as the name implies. The shuttle is struck by the player with the racket, usually below the height of the net, and the flight of the shuttle goes up the side of the net, over the top, and then down on the other side. The success of this shot lies in the element of surprise and also in the intended low net clearance of the shuttle. Remember that it is not necessary to allow the shuttle to fall away from the top of the net, before returning it to the opponent. If you can reach the shuttle early, just block it back for a drop shot, or quickly punch it for a winner. The hairpin is used for shots that are reached late, after the shuttle has descended below the height of the net.

Hairpin drop shot

Hairpin drop shot
using the forehand

Hairpin drop shot
using the backhand

As you prepare to hit the hairpin drop, the grip may be maintained as prescribed for drives, or it may be somewhat shortened to establish more control. Practice will determine which is more satisfactory, as either is appropriate.

For purposes of disguise, basic footwork should remain the same as for drives and clears. As the shuttle approaches, quickly place the racket face directly beneath the descending shuttle, and carefully contact it with just enough force to reach the height of the net. Try to glide the shuttle over the net, rather than hitting it. Aim the shuttle slightly forward to cause it to descend on the other side of the net once sufficient height has been achieved. Be sure to watch the shuttle into the strings of your racket to secure good contact.

In all drop shots, the element of surprise is paramount in your strategy. Therefore, do not telegraph your intentions to an opponent. Mix your drops with a generous supply of drives, smashes and deep clears, using the same backswing motion with all. This will keep your opponent guessing at all times.

Once the hairpin drop is completed, remember to recover to your home position, so you can adequately cover all parts of the court.

The Cross-Court Drop

As you may have already guessed, this drop shot moves diagonally across the net to the other side, maintaining a low flight, barely clearing the net, and rapidly descending on the other side. The basic grips are the same as those used with the hairpin drop. The higher you are able to contact the shuttle in the cross-court drop, the more apt you are to have a successful stroke.

As the shuttle approaches, having descended low over the net and to one side, you must quickly approach the shuttle with your racket at the ready position. Placing the racket below and away from the side you intend to direct your drop, quickly glide the racket through the shot, finishing with a long follow-through, assuring complete control of the stroke. As the shuttle leaves the racket, it should rise quickly toward the top of the net, barely clear the top, and fall quickly on the other side. **A word of caution:** Whenever you raise the flight of the shuttle more than six inches above the net after hitting a drop shot, your opponent may charge the shuttle and drive it quickly at you or at an open part of your court. Keep it low! At the completion of the stroke, quickly recover to your home position.

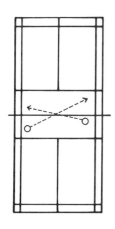

Cross-court dropshot
(keep low and short)

Cross-court drop shot, showing forehand (top) and backhand (bottom)

The Overhead Drop

The success of this stroke, as with many others, lies in your ability to disguise the shot. When a shuttle is flying overhead, a skilled player can hit a clear, smash, drive or a drop shot. As you prepare to hit the shuttle, you alone know the shot you plan to use. That is, in your mind you already know which stroke you plan to use, so don't change your mind unless your opponent commits toward that part of the court early.

As you prepare to hit the overhead drop shot, remember where you are on the court and where your opponent is located. Aim your shot to the open forecourt. The photos above illustrate the intended target area.

Duplicate the normal backswing preparation as though you are preparing to hit a deep clear or a smash. In all probability, your opponent will read this into the shot and begin to back up. As you bring the racket forward to the contact point, high and slightly out in front of the body, start to slow the racket head dramatically as you approach the shuttle. Upon contact, follow through only slightly as you complete the stroke. This will allow the stroke to appear as a strong, deep shot, while in reality the shuttle barely clears the net, descending rapidly. Practice will give you much needed confidence in using the overhead clear in your game. It is a fantastic point winner, but remember that deception is the key to success.

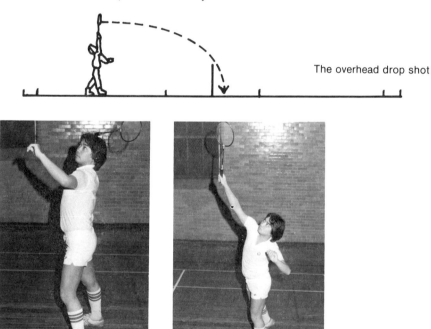

The overhead drop shot

Overhead drop shot: **Left,** preparation; **Right,** contact area

The Underhand Drop

This is another frequently used shot that is a surprise stroke, and is almost totally defensive, since the shuttle must be stroked upwards. The underhand drop can best be described as a shot hit with the wrist in a laid-back position. The correct grip and wrist position are illustrated in the accompanying photograph.

As the shuttle descends in your forecourt, quickly move into position and place the racket head beneath it. Using only a slight wrist motion, slowly guide the shuttle back across the net, keeping it low and allowing it to drop rapidly. Although similar to the hairpin drop, the underhand drop is made from farther back in the area of the short service line. You will probably experience more success with these shots on the forehand side than the backhand, due primarily to the nature of the wrist position.

Wrist position for the underhand drop

Drops are great fun to add to the game. Most skilled players spend many hours practicing them so that both disguise and accuracy can be achieved. Once you have accomplished sufficient skill in all of the drop shots, you will have developed an aggressive, exciting dimension to your strategy. Keep working at them, and you will be very satisfied with the results.

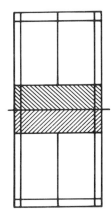

Target areas for drop shots (use alleys for doubles)

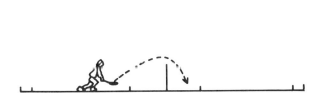

Underhand drop shot

Tips on Drop Shot Technique

1. Determine in your mind which shot you plan to use, then GO FOR IT!
2. Shorten the grip slightly when preparing for the hairpin drop, as this will give you greater control.
3. Remember that disguise is most important in maintaining the element of surprise.
4. When stroking the hairpin and cross-court drops, keep the wrist in the laid-back position and well under control.
5. Use proper footwork whenever possible, as this will place you in the best position to execute your shot.
6. Be careful to mix your drops with other types of shots and do not rely on them totally. Keeping the opponent off balance and unable to anticipate your strategy, will give you the edge.
7. Make your racket preparation the same for all overhead strokes — drops included.
8. Recover promptly to your home position to achieve adequate court coverage at all times.
9. Keep alert to your opponent's court position, as this will dictate where your next shot should go.
10. KEEP YOUR DROP SHOT LOW!

Name_____

Chapter 10 Evaluation

1. Why is deception such an important part of playing the net?

2. On one stroke, it is recommended that you shorten the grip on the racket. Which stroke uses this procedure?

3. Of the four types of drop shots covered, which is the most deceptive? Why?

4. Explain the use of the wrist in stroking drop shots. Some use the wrist greatly, others not at all. Why?

5. Why is retrieving a well-executed drop shot so difficult? What shots would you use to counter this stroke?

6. How does the hairpin drop differ from the cross-court drop?

(Over)

7. The height that the shuttle clears the net on a drop shot is very important. Why?

8. How could a receiver block a drop shot back to the opposing player? Is this good strategy?

9. Would returning a short serve in singles with a drop shot be a good strategic move? Why or why not?

Chapter 11

The Clears

As in most racket sports, certain strokes are used for specific purposes. Such is the case for the clear. The word "clear" is an accurate description, since the properly executed stroke goes over the opponent ("clears" the opponent) and drops behind in an open part of the court.

Usually the stroke is used as a defensive shot, as it drives the opponent back from an attack position. However, if the opposing player has a backhand weakness, then the clear may be used as an attack stroke, allowing the clearing player to mount the offensive.

Probably the greatest problem for most players is the shot which is deep to the backhand, going over the head of the player, and landing in the far rear corner. This can be compounded by the high trajectory, which prevents the receiver from contacting the shuttle until it is deep in the backcourt.

The clear may be hit on the forehand or the backhand side, as an overhead or as an underhand stroke. You might draw a comparison to the high deep serve used in singles. This is actually an underhand clear, used to back the opponent to the rear of the receiving court, on the defensive, if possible.

Generally, the forehand side is the easier shot, because most players are stronger on this side than on the backhand. Since this is recognized by both opponents, most high clears will be directed at the backhand side. This is to be expected as a planned attack by an aggressive opponent, so a strong defense is needed to thwart this attack.

As you prepare to hit a clear, remember that a low clear is not called a clear, but a set-up. Be sure to plan for height and depth; otherwise you may find yourself on the short end of a smash.

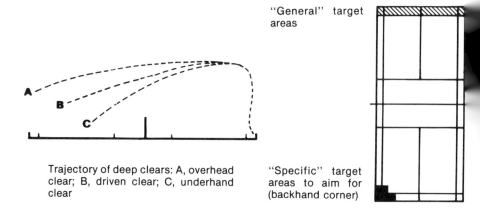

"General" target areas

Trajectory of deep clears: A, overhead clear; B, driven clear; C, underhand clear

"Specific" target areas to aim for (backhand corner)

The Underhand Clear

The description of the underhand clear is almost identical to the high deep serve in singles. You must assume the correct forehand grip and adjust your feet to allow you to step into the shuttle when the flight causes the bird to reach a point just in front of the forward knee. Aim high and deep, toward the backhand corner. The force with which you hit should include a shift of body weight and arm and wrist action. Your footwork causes you to turn your side slightly to the net, making it easier to aim the forward stroke. The follow-through should be complete, finishing high with the racket above the left shoulder. Quickly recover to place yourself in a ready position for the next shot.

The Overhead Clear

This stroke has many possibilities. As an overhead stroke, the preparatory motion is the same as a smash, drive, drop shot or a clear. Thus you keep your opponent wondering which shot you are going to hit next, and the variety keeps him/her off balance.

As you prepare to hit the overhead clear, slightly turn your side to the net, and bring the racket back into the full backswing position. (See the photos on the opposite page.) Be sure to have a good forehand grip on the handle of the racket, and position yourself so that the shuttle is always slightly in front of your body. As the shuttle comes within reach, extend the racket up into the shuttle, contacting it with an open face and directing the flight toward the opponent's deep backcourt. Be sure to aim high and deep to

THE OVERHEAD CLEAR SEQUENCE

clear the opponent's racket. REMEMBER: the shuttle is light and you are hitting it a great distance, so don't hold back on your swing. Gauge the shot according to your position on the court, adjusting the force of the shot to your position.

Explosive power is particularly needed if you are near the center of your court or in the backcourt area, since you must drive the shuttle a great distance to keep the opponent from mounting an offensive. Remember, this shot requires force to drive the shuttle into the backcourt area of your opponent.

As the shuttle approaches, whip the racket through the shuttle, leading with the head of the racket and contacting the shuttle in front of the body and slightly out in front. Time your stroke to reach maximum power upon contact. As you meet the shuttle at arm's length, increase the wrist rotation to accelerate the speed of the racket head. Finish the stroke with a rapid follow-through and a quick recovery.

The Backhand Clear

The backhand clear may possibly be the most important stroke in badminton. This is due to the weakness found in many players for this particular shot. Proper form and technique will help most players overcome the problem, but considerable practice is needed to master this stroke.

As you see the shuttle approach, quickly change to the backhand grip, with the thumb along the back side of the handle. Keep the shuttle in front of the body and turn your side to the net, with weight on the rear foot. As the racket is cocked, bend the elbow, and tighten up slightly on the grip. As the shuttle approaches the point of contact, quickly whip the racket face upward and forward, contacting it at a high, comfortable reach. As the forward stroke is made with the racket, shift the weight forward into the stroke. Hit through the shuttle, utilizing the wrist to give maximum momentum to the racket head. Follow through in the desired direction of the shuttle flight and recover quickly for the return shot.

To gain proficiency in this stroke requires considerable practice to achieve sufficient strength for proper height and depth. Don't give up or become discouraged, for once you have mastered this one, the rest will seem easy.

THE BACKHAND CLEAR SEQUENCE

THE UNDERHAND BACKHAND CLEAR SEQUENCE

The Underhand Backhand Clear

When executing the backhand clear, it is best to utilize the backhand grip described earlier. When you realize the shuttle is to your backhand, but low, move up to the bird to prevent it from dropping too low, and prepare your backswing as you have practiced in the previous stroke. As the shuttle approaches the contact point, bend the knees to position the racket head under the shuttle and, in a long, low-to-high sweeping motion, swish the racket head through the shot, accelerating the wrist as you proceed. Be sure to flex the wrist to give additional speed to the face of the racket.

Tips on Technique for the Clear

1. Move into position quickly, changing grips when necessary as you move.
2. Always try to keep the shuttle in front of you.
3. Remember — height plus depth!
4. Be sure to keep the thumb print along the back side of the racket handle.
5. Step into the stroke as you make contact with the shuttle.
6. Rotate the wrist through the stroke as contact is made.
7. Aim most clears toward your opponent's backhand corner.
8. Practice this stroke often, as it is your "bread and butter" shot.
9. Use proper footwork at all times, since it will make a big difference in your stroke.
10. As you complete your backswing for the backhand stroke, be sure your elbow is pointed towards the shuttle.

Name_____

Chapter 11 Evaluation

1. Why is the clear such an important shot in the game of badminton?

2. Success is greatly aided by keeping the shuttle in front of the body. Why?

3. What strategy is used when hitting the clear?

4. Why is the singles serve considered a clear?

5. Explain the strategy used in the height and depth theory.

6. How does "aiming the elbow" at the shuttle aid you in making a better stroke?

7. Why does the thumb play such an important part in the backhand grip used for the backhand clear?

8. Explain the theory that the backhand clear is the weakest for the average badminton player.

Chapter 12

The Smash

No stroke in the game of badminton is as spectacular as the smash. Since the player uses the smash to win a point, it is hit quite forcefully. If hit correctly at the proper time, the plan usually holds true. Although the shuttle may travel at a high rate of speed, it decelerates rapidly, so a sharp downward angle is very important. The speed of the shot is most helpful in achieving desired results, but the angle is equally as important.

Unlike other strokes, such as clears, drives and drop shots, this stroke is a total overhead shot. To achieve perfection, the stroke must be hit from a position halfway back in the court to the net — the closer the better. Remember that the net is five feet high at the center, so you have to reach high when contacting the shuttle to drive it at the desired angle.

As you prepare to stroke the shuttle with an overhead smash, you should position yourself so that the shuttle remains slightly in front of your body. Quickly analyze the incoming shuttle to decide which type of return to use. Once you decide to use the smash, go for it!

Turn your side to the net, and use the side-stepping motion to achieve proper positioning. As you glide under the shuttle, be sure to keep the bird slightly in front of your body. Tighten your forehand grip on the handle of the racket to secure it, and quickly bring the racket into the full backswing position behind the back as in the accompanying photo. Remember that you can now hit four different strokes — the clear, drop, drive or smash — from this position. Your opponent, also realizing this, will be uncertain about which area to cover unless you give away your intentions.

Preparation for the smash

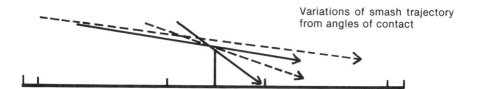

Variations of smash trajectory
from angles of contact

As the shuttle approaches, shift your weight to the rear foot, to enable you to shift forward and unleash more power into the stroke. Remember you must catch the shuttle at its highest possible point to achieve the best downward angle. Now quickly whip the racket head upward into the descending shuttle, contacting it with a closed racket face pointed slightly downward. The sharpness of the angle will be determined somewhat by your position on the court. The closer you are to the net, the greater the downward angle. The farther you are from the net, the less the angle will be.

When you contact the shuttle, be sure to rotate the forearm and the wrist completely and shift your weight forward into the shot. Go for the winner, but recover quickly to play any successful return. Your follow-through will be short, and you should visibly follow the flight of the shuttle so you can counter any return.

An experienced player will work the opponent with a series of shots to open up the opportunity to use the smash. A combination of drives, clears, and drops will cause the opponent to move about extensively, thus opening up areas of attack.

SMASH SEQUENCE

BACKHAND SMASH

The Backhand Smash

This is a variation of the overhead smash, but comes on the backhand side. It should be used when you lack sufficient time to move around the shuttle for a forehand shot. This stroke is most successful when you are very close to the net.

As the shuttle approaches, quickly change grips, and bring the racket into the backswing position (for backhands). Quickly stroke the shuttle at a sharp downward angle, placing the thumb behind the grip to accelerate the racket head. Be sure to contact the shuttle well in front of the body, and have your right side turned toward the net for proper results.

Most players usually acquire success with this stroke after a few hours of practice.

Tips on Technique for the Smash

1. Move the opponent about the playing area, using a variety of shots, to open up areas of the court for the smash.
2. Plan your smash and aim it toward the open court.
3. Tighten your grip to secure the racket in your hand.
4. Keep slightly behind the shuttle as it descends.
5. Reach high to contact the shuttle.
6. Rotate the arm and the wrist fully when contacting the shuttle.
7. If possible, shift your weight into the stroke.
8. Turn your left side to the net to allow you to hit across the body, thus giving more acceleration to the stroke.

Name_____

Chapter 12 Evaluation

1. Why is the angle of the smash so vitally important to the success of the stroke?

2. Should you use an open, closed, or flat racket face when you contact the shuttle?

3. How does deception play an important part in the execution of the smash?

4. Explain the relationship between your position on the court and the success of the smash.

5. Why is the backhand smash most successful closer to the net?

6. Which grip is recommended for stroking the smash?

Chapter 13

The Round-The-Head Shot

The round-the-head shot is just what it implies. You are stroking the shuttle around the other side of your head. If you are right-handed, you will hit the shuttle above your left shoulder, and if left-handed, it will be just the opposite.

At times it is necessary to maintain the attack even though you may be forced to hit a shot from an awkward position. The round-the-head is the type of shot for these situations. The types of shots frequently hit from the round-the-head positon are drives, drops, half-smashes, and clears. In other words, there are many varieties that may be used from this basic stroke.

As the shuttle approaches, and you find yourself in the position of being forced to hit the round-the-head shot, you must quickly react by adjusting your feet, acquiring your balance, and shifting to the forehand grip or (if you feel more comfortable and controlled) the shortened grip. Keeping the shuttle in front of the body, quickly take the racket on the backswing behind the back, and whip the racket head over the top of your head and through the shuttle. Utilize the wrist as you make contact with the shuttle, and keep your follow-through as short as you can in order to recover quickly and maintain body balance for the possible return shot.

At the instant of contact, the racket face should be flat against the shuttle to allow maximum strength to flow into the force of the stroke.

Use caution in attempting shots that are well to the left side of the body. Since it is a difficult stroke at best, and one that many novice players will have trouble with, don't overdo the reach extension of the racket.

When low trajectory shots are hit toward you, you must bend the knees slightly to get under the shot. Many round-the-head shots are contacted just

ROUND-THE-HEAD-SHOT

above the left shoulder rather than in front of it. This is quite common since the adjustment period involves valuable time which allows the shuttle to penetrate more deeply toward you.

This stroke will demand quite a lot of practice, and can best be achieved with drills utilizing a feeder for practice. Be sure to give this shot plenty of respect, but once again, you will find that practice will make it much easier.

Tips on Technique for the Round-the-head Shot

1. Adjust your footwork quickly for balance and stability.
2. Change your grip to that of your choice (regular or shortened).
3. Keep your eye on the shuttle at all times.
4. Be very conscious of not allowing the shuttle to get behind you.
5. Contact the shuttle with a flat racket face.
6. Utilize the wrist strongly when hitting the shuttle.
7. Follow-through quickly and recover immediately.

Name_____

Chapter 13 Evaluation

1. Why do you think this shot is more difficult than some of the others?

2. Which grip will give you more control? Why?

3. What is the stroking procedure for the low trajectory return coming in close to your body?

4. What type of strokes can be hit from the round-the-head position?

5. Explain your body position when forced to hit this shot.

6. Should your racket face be open, flat or closed at contact? Why?

7. Why is the round-the-head shot preferable to a backhand stroke?

Chapter 14

Singles Strategy

Webster defines the word "strategy" as the "employment of means on a broad scale for gaining advantage of an opponent." In badminton, this may be interpreted as "using skill and tactics to establish and maintain total control of the game." Strategy is often as important as ability. When two opponents are equally skilled and properly conditioned, then the deployment of strategy may be **more** important in achieving a victory than skill.

Strategy is based upon such factors as confidence, skill development, conditioning, knowledge of the game, execution of techniques, determination, and other elements that are used in championship athletics. Let's examine some of these to see how they fit into the definition of strategy.

Physical Conditioning

The most important element of the game, with the exception of skill, is physical conditioning. Many young badminton players are unfamiliar with the quality and pace the game demands. It is known to be the fastest net game in the world. Once the novice player sees championship badminton being played, then a deeper appreciation for physical stamina is forthcoming.

To be properly conditioned for badminton, you must develop a training program that will establish total fitness. This will include muscular strength as well as cardiovascular endurance, since both play an important part in badminton. Running, weight training, rope skipping, sprints, "shadow drills" for footwork, reaction drills, and many others greatly enhance your ability to get to the shuttle early, make adequate preparations, and properly execute the correct stroke.

Remember that once you tire your strokes become weaker, especially those that demand quick reaction and movement. Probably one of the first strokes to indicate this will be the backhand clear. If you fail to move into position quickly, your shot will become shallow. Instead of driving your opponent away from the attack position, the opponent will move in for the kill.

As you begin to tire due to excess movement and running, you will be late for many shots, your returns will be weaker, and you will have difficulty in moving up and back and from side to side. If this happens, you are where your opponent wants you — always on the defensive and unable to defend against the attack. There is no defense against physical fatigue, so you must condition yourself to play the game.

Skill Development

While skill development and physical conditioning go hand in hand, you will become very frustrated if you get to the shuttle but cannot adequately work the stroke to set up a winner. There are many strokes in the game and all of them are important. There is a counter shot for every offensive ploy your opponent may attempt.

Championship players spend hours developing, conditioning, and refining stroke techniques. This is what athletics and competion are all about: to find your game and then work hard (physically and mentally) to develop it to its maximum. The more you work, the better you become; the better you become, the more you want to play.

All badminton strokes are designed for specific purposes. Serves are used not only to put the shuttle into play, but also to keep you out of trouble at that critical time. Drives are used to keep your opponent off-balance. Clears are used to move your opponent away from the home position and on the defensive. They are also used to give you more time to recover when necessary.

Because your enjoyment of the game will largely depend on your skill level, you should take the time to learn the skills thoroughly. Then practice so you can use them whenever needed.

Mental Development

Mental development is not just an appreciation of the game of badminton, but the development of a mental attitude that will detect an opponent's weaknesses and show you the offensive strategy to use to win the contest.

When you condition yourself properly, learn to execute the strokes of the game adequately, and practice sufficiently to maintain your skill at peak performance, you acquire that magical feeling of **confidence** — the extra edge needed for success.

Success also requires dedication and discipline. Many players want to be successful but are not willing to pay the price for the excellence. It is not easy, for it must be achieved through hard work. However, badminton is fun, and this makes us want to become better. Humans are competitive by nature. We have been instilled with the competitive philosophy throughout our lives — in school, on the playground, at home, at work and in athletics. It is a purpose for practice.

Developing a positive mental attitude about your game, backed by hard work and discipline, will enable you to challenge with confidence — and win!

Offensive Techniques

A learned person once said, when speaking of the game of badminton, that the way to play is to "hit 'em hard, and wish 'em well!" While this might work most of the time, it is not sound advice to follow in all situations. When developing offensive strategy, you must understand how to benefit from the element of surprise, and how to disguise various shots to prevent your opponent from determining your intentions. Hitting the shuttle the same way every time will simply enable you to lose at a faster pace. Skilled performers will quickly anticipate those shots, and move to counter them with techniques that will place you in untenable situations.

Serving Strategy

The basic serve for singles is the high, deep serve. The purpose of this stroke is to put your opponent on the defensive immediately. By placing the serve deep into the receiver's backcourt and to the backhand, you move the player to a deep position where no offensive stroke can be offered. Also, you now have your opponent in a situation where the **best** stroke that can be hit is to clear the shuttle deep to **your** backcourt. This is a difficult serve for your opponent for two reasons: (1) it is a considerable distance to your backcourt — forty-four feet; and (2) immediately after serving, you have recovered to your home position, centrally located in your court. This position enables you to reach most shuttles without giving away your court position. Not so with your opponent, since the shuttle is being hit with a backhand return which is usually weaker than the forehand.

Stroke flight description

1. Hairpin Drop
2. Underhand Drop
3. Short Low Serve
4. High Deep Serve
5. Deep Clear
6. Drive (FH or BH)
7. Smash

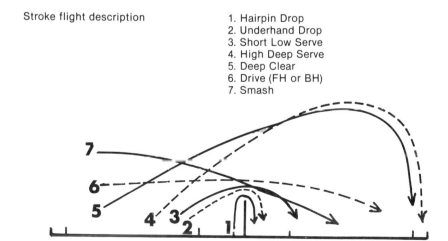

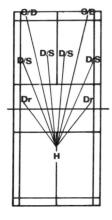
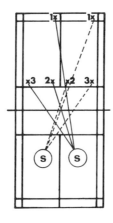
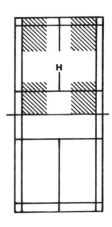

| Stroke variety from midcourt C = Clear; D = Drive; S = Smash; Dr = Drop; H = Home Position | Serve variations (Short and low or high and deep) 1 = Best;   2 = Good; 3 = Fair | Hit to the open area — away from home |

Variations of the serve, such as serving deep to the forehand, for a change of pace will also strengthen your game. In addition, using a short serve to the forehand and backhand corner to catch an opponent off-guard will sometimes produce desired results. Remember, however, that the basic, standard serve for singles is the high deep serve, which forces the opponent away from the net and attacking position.

There are occasions when you might wish to stand in the corner of the singles court nearer the sideline when serving. While this may catch the novice by surprise, it is easily countered by the skilled player, causing the server to be immediately placed on the defensive. Some benefit might result on the forehand side, when serving to the deep backhand corner, using either a drive serve or a high deep serve. Generally, however, this position is not recommended for the server.

Keeping the Point Alive

Keep the shuttle in play until the moment when you can go for a winner. Don't make careless mistakes as you play. In viewing a game, it often seems as though most points are won by someone making an error, such as hitting the shuttle in the net or out of bounds, rather than the point being won by a placement. This is usually true, for until consistency is developed, many errors will occur.

Simple strategy concepts, such as hitting the shuttle away from the opponent and toward the open court, are very valuable. A player has a far better chance to make an error when he/she must cover the entire court, so stroke the bird to the open areas and move them.

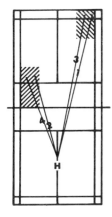

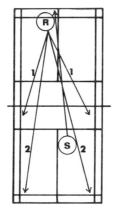

Mix your shots to run
your opponent

Service returns
1 = drop; 2 = clear

BISECTING THE ANGLES OF RETURN

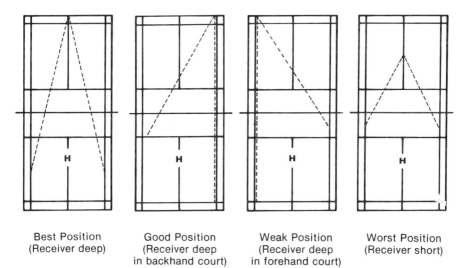

| Best Position (Receiver deep) | Good Position (Receiver deep in backhand court) | Weak Position (Receiver deep in forehand court) | Worst Position (Receiver short) |

Keeping the Shuttle Low

This is one of the basic rules of strategy. Since the net is five feet high in the center, all strategy is developed with this in mind. Whenever possible, drive the shuttle downward toward your opponent's court. There is little chance that you will win the point against a good opponent when you hit the shuttle at an upward angle. Granted there are times when you can simply drive the shuttle past the player and beat him/her to the backcourt with the speed of the bird, but usually this is not possible.

By hitting the shuttle downward whenever possible and practical, you force the opponent to lift the shuttle to get it over the net. This provides the opportunity to hit the shuttle with an occasional smash, drop shot, drive, or any shot you might select.

Mixing Your Shots

Drop shots and clears will force your opponent to move the entire length of the court (22 feet). While this is not a great distance, causing your opponent to do this several times for every point will soon open court areas for a kill shot. Also, occasional drives to keep an opponent off-balance will make your job easier.

Remember your angles of return. The best angle is from the center of the opponent's backcourt. This provides the best possible area to cover the return shot. Your home position is in the center of the court, about five feet behind the short service line. The angles can be covered better from this position than any other.

Use Disguise Whenever Possible

Deception is an integral part of badminton. Since several strokes can originate from one typical backswing position, you must keep your opponent guessing which one you will hit. Will it be a drop, smash, drive or clear? You are the only one who knows for sure, so use as much variety as possible to force an opening. Keep your attack alive with a mixture of shots.

Defensive Strategy

Defensive shots are usually hit with an upward angle to clear the net or to provide time to recover to your home position. These are the serves, clears, underhand drops and drives with a trajectory from low to high.

When playing defensively, the basic shot pattern will be the drop-clear strategy. This will make your opponent cover as much court as possible, moving deep for the clear and returning quickly for the drop shot. This will also force an opponent to lift the drop shot or to return the high clear from deep backcourt, taking you off the defensive, and opening up offensive opportunities. Drops may be countered with either hairpin drops or deep clears. A smash may be returned with a drop or a deep clear.

Be alert when you play. Try to read your opponent's intentions. If your opponent smashes from the baseline, the shuttle will slow sufficiently for you to handle it when it reaches your court. If your opponent anticipates that you will drop shot, hold your intentions a little longer until the opponent is committed, then flick with a deep clear. This will cause great difficulty for any opponent.

Most players tend to be either offensively oriented, or defensive in their style of play. Some go both ways, defending when necessary and attacking whenever possible. There is no established rule or procedure. Both are excellent strategies, as the defensive player will generate points by causing the opponent to make errors, and the offensive player will make points by attacking.

Tips on Singles Strategy

1. Develop a high deep serve that is accurate and moves your opponent as deep as possible in the receiving court.

2. A short serve should be stroked exactly as the deep serve for disguise.

3. Return short serves with drop or clear.

4. Return high deep serves with a clear, half smash, or drop.

5. Establish a strategy for your style of play and develop the skill to implement it.

6. If you are losing, change your style of play. Stay with your game plan if you are winning.

7. Disguise your stroke whenever possible to keep your opponent guessing.

8. Mix your shots to keep your opponent running as much as possible.

9. Return the opponent's smash with a drop or clear.

10. Bisect the angle of return if possible.

11. Be properly conditioned for aggressive singles play.

Name_____

Chapter 14 Evaluation

1. Which serve is best when playing singles. Why?

2. When is the short service useful? The driven serve?

3. Which strokes are used predominately in singles?

4. Why is conditioning such an important part of badminton?

5. Where is your home position when receiving service in the left service court?

6. When driven to the backcourt to retrieve a deep clear, which shots would you use to return the shuttle?

7. Outline a combination of shots that would illustrate singles strategy during a point.

8. What part dooo mental strategy play in your game? How do you build this?

(Over)

9. How does deception play into your strategy?

10. When we speak of hitting the shuttle downward whenever possible, we are indicating a strategy procedure. Explain.

Chapter 15

Doubles Strategy

Doubles is a team game, requiring concentrated effort on the part of both players to maximize skill and coordinate effort. Partners must play together regularly to assess their strengths and weaknesses. A good doubles team harmonizes and blends into an effective mold for maximum results.

Personality makeup is also very important in the selection of a partner. Ideally partners should be able to complement the personalities and skills of each other as well as have a thorough understanding of the game. Doubles is a good way to capitalize on your finer playing points and to disguise your weaknesses from the opponents. Choose a partner who has good stroke execution, is physically conditioned, understands the theory of good doubles play and is compatible to you. These qualities, along with continual team play, will result in a formidable doubles team.

DOUBLES FORMATION

The three basic formations for doubles are (1) Side-by-side; (2) Up and back; and (3) Rotation — a combination of the first two formations. A knowledge of these three formations will provide you with an understanding of the concepts behind doubles strategy.

Side-by-Side

In this formation both partners play side by side, with each covering half of the court from the net to the back boundary line, and from the center line to the doubles sideline. This is an excellent formation, and is easy to understand from the viewpoint of court coverage. It is strong against an attacking team and is very difficult to smash through, due to the complete coverage of the court at the center.

SIDE-BY-SIDE FORMATION

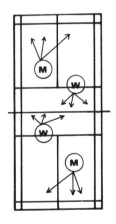

Mixed doubles
positions

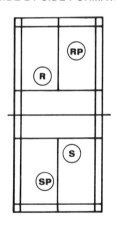

Service and receiving
positions

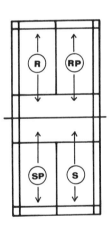

Court coverage respon-
sibilities

When using this formation, it is usually best to place the player with the weakest backhand on the right side. Although you will change places as the game progresses, at least fifty percent of the time the player who is weak on the backhand will have partner's forehand for support when retrieving deep drives and clears.

However, there are several disadvantages in the side-by-side system. For instance, if one partner has a blatant deficiency, it will be easier for the opponents to play that person and exploit the weakness, since it is not a difficult task to keep the shuttle directed toward this player. Also, it is much easier to use the drop-clear strategy to run the player and intentionally keep the other partner away from the shuttle. Thus, the player receiving most shots may likely be the one the opponents have determined to be the weaker of the team. A direct result of this strategy is that the weaker player will tire more quickly, and begin to open areas of attack because of weak returns.

Up and Back

The up and back system is just what the title implies — one partner plays up (close to the net) and the other partner covers the backcourt area. This formation usually works well for partners who frequently play together, since it requires close harmony for each to understand the other's responsibility.

The up, or net, person is usually the player who is serving or receiving. The other partner covers all deep shots. When playing mixed doubles, the female usually plays the net position and her male counterpart covers the backcourt.

The up and back formation can accentuate the strengths of a good team and protect possible weaknesses due to the placement of the partners. The team which can drive the shuttle downward will be the attacking team. By placing one partner close to the net, careless or weakly hit shuttles can easily be cut off and punched for a winner. The stronger player in the backcourt can direct play from this position by using drops and high-to-low drives which will cause the opponents to hit at an upward angle, enabling the attacking team to score more easily.

UP AND BACK FORMATION

Up and Back Formation

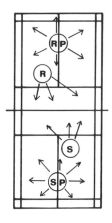

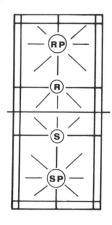

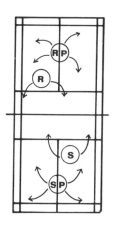

Serving and receiving

Playing responsibilities

Rotation system
roving responsibilities

Serving Positions for Partners

The basic weakness of this system lies in the possibility of the sidelines being vulnerable for well placed shots, since both players play close to the
center line to cover the angles of attack.

Rotation

The rotation system is simply a combination of the side-by-side and the up and back system. Obviously there are distinct advantages in roaming about the open court, since the opponents have no fixed target of attack. In actuality, however, the flow of the game greatly determines where you will be playing. If your partner goes up, you cover the backcourt, and vice versa.

When you are defending, you should immediately switch to a side-by-side formation to deter the attack. When you are on the attack, you should go to the up and back formation, since you have more opportunity at the net to put the point away.

In adjusting to the rotation system, the server (or the receiver) determines who plays each position. For example, since the basic serve in doubles is a low service, the server covers the net to protect against a drop return. The receiver who receives a low serve, may in turn cover the net since this serve will keep them there. The partner covers the backcourt area.

If the service is a driven serve, forcing the receiver deep toward the rear of the court, the receiver should return the shuttle and remain in the backcourt area. The partner of the receiver then covers the forecourt (net) area. The secret is coordination of effort with each partner understanding his or her responsibility and knowing what to do in a given situation. This produces a winning doubles team.

Remember that the up and back formation works best when on the attack. When defending, always drop back into a side-by-side formation to provide greater coverage against the smash.

SERVING

The basic serve in doubles is the short, low serve! There is a good reason for this. First of all, the court is two and a half feet shorter than the singles court, making the high deep serve very short, so the smash becomes a very appropriate shot as a service return.

A good low serve barely clears the net and drops quickly into the receivers' court to the short service line. The best placement will be exactly in the corner, where the short service line touches the center line. For variety, the server may direct the serve to the wide corner, where the short service line bisects the doubles sideline. Be careful not to hit out of bounds, or to land short.

High short serves will be challenged by the opponent at the net and will be driven straight at you, usually causing a loss of service. Remember — if you serve short, serve low.

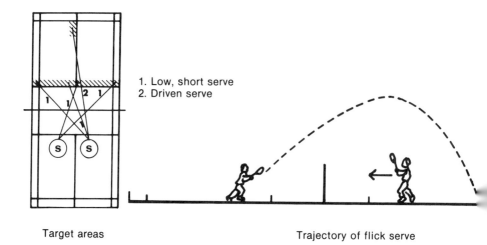

1. Low, short serve
2. Driven serve

Target areas   Trajectory of flick serve

The Driven Serve

This serve is highly deceptive, for it appears to be identical to all the other serves. The preparation is exactly the same as the short serve. However, instead of serving short and low, the shuttle is driven in a flat trajectory, usually at the backhand corner. Surprise is the key element, and you often win the point outright by catching an opponent off-balance. Use this serve sparingly for a quick change of pace. It can be very successful for you.

The Flick Serve

Probably every experienced badminton player has been caught in the embarrassing position caused by a flick serve. Once you realize you are the victim, there is little chance to recover, since your opponent has the advantage and frequently the point.

Most experienced players use the flick serve as a strategic weapon. It is usually stroked with a backhand grip by holding the shuttle in front of the body (keeping in mind the rules for serving). The flick serve motion is used sparingly as the short low serve dominates. However, for a change of pace, the shuttle is flicked over the head of the opponent, high enough to be out of reach and deep enough to drop behind the receiver.

Many players like to charge the serve, and since most serves in doubles are short and low, the receiver can often block the shot for a winner. The server must anticipate this move to be successful with the flick serve. The server is like a quarterback, who, reading a blitz, counters with a play to catch the defense flat-footed. This is when the flick serve is most successful. As the aggressive receiver charges what is thought to be a short low serve, the server, anticipating the charge, flicks the shuttle over the charger's head out of reach for a winner.

Flick serve   Mixed doubles, flick serve   Mixed doubles, regular serve

THE RETURN OF SERVE

You cannot score points when receiving a service. Therefore, you must defend against the serve to win back the opportunity to put your game plan to work. Thus the return of service is very important.

Since most doubles serves are short and low, your choice of return lies with either a drop shot (straight ahead, not a cross-court), a drive, or a "push shot" either directly at the server or the partner.

Drop Returns

If you elect to drop shot a return of service, you must keep the shuttle low as it passes over the net. If the server has a habit of stepping backward after serving, a drop shot to the open area directly in front of you will usually win the point. Drop shots must have a trajectory that will keep them within three or four inches above the net. Also, the closer your return shot drops to the net the better, since their return shot will have to be almost straight up, giving you the attack.

Drive Returns

Using a drive as a return of serve can be very successful, especially if the drive is well placed and near the far backhand corner of the court. The return speed of the shuttle causes the serving team great difficulty in obtaining position for a successful return of the drive and causes confusion as to proper court coverage. Usually drive returns to the backhand side are far more successful than those to the forehand, or strong side.

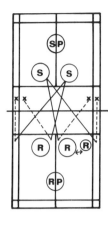 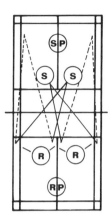

Drop return of service   Drive return of service

Push return

Remember if you are receiving a short low serve, you will likely be driving the shuttle in a low-to-high trajectory, so you must be careful. If you lift it too high, your opponent will simply smash it at you.

Push Returns

Push returns are used when the shuttle is high enough to give the receiver a line of flight either straight ahead or slightly downward. As the shuttle travels across the net, a high trajectory will enable the receiver to begin an effective attack or to win the point outright.

Any shuttle that is six to ten inches above the net on a short service should be immediately attacked. As the shuttle clears the net, quickly move forward and punch the shuttle directly at the right shoulder of the server or to an open part of the court. Aiming the shuttle directly at the server causes much distress, and after a few shots, the server becomes greatly intimidated. This insecurity then causes the serving team to lower the trajectory of the serve, thus causing many service attempts to land in the net.

Doubles is a tremendous game, and much pleasure can be derived by those who learn to play it well. Remember that it requires a team effort, and the greater the harmony between partners, the more successful your team will be.

Tips on Techniques for Doubles Play

1. Select a compatible partner.
2. Play together enough to know the strengths and weaknesses of both partners.
3. Learn the strategy associated with the various doubles formations.
4. Learn the strokes that are predominantly used in doubles, and practice them enough to become proficient.
5. When playing mixed doubles, put the female in the forecourt position.
6. Determine the weaker of the opponents and direct most of your play to that person whenever possible.
7. Know the weaknesses of each doubles formation and use them against your opponents.
8. Use the flick and drive serves with discretion.
9. Keep the shuttle on a high-to-low trajectory whenever possible to maintain the attack.
10. Practice, Practice, Practice your service, drops, drives, and smashes. Remember that practice is the key to success.

Name_____

Chapter 15 Evaluation

1. Briefly name and describe the various formations used in doubles play.

2. In your opinion, which formation would be the best to use?

3. Why is the low service used predominantly in doubles?

4. Explain the service courts. How do they differ from singles?

5. In mixed doubles, where should the female play?

6. What are the advantages of the side-by-side formation?

7. Which options are suggested when receiving a smash?

(Over)

8. When does the flick service come into play?

9. What is a push shot and how is it applied to doubles?

10. When can you charge the service? Is this a good move? What are the disadvantages?

Chapter 16

Practice Drills

Practice is essential for mastery of badminton skills and good practice habits should be established early in the learning process. Several characteristics distinguish good from bad practice.

First of all, the practice needs a definite purpose and focus. A specific skill should be identified and the drill selected should allow for many repetitions of that particular skill.

Secondly, the drill needs to be appropriate to the skill level of the player. One theory suggests that the best learning occurs when there is a 90% success rate. This means that the drill or task selected must be easy enough for the learner to correctly execute nine of every ten attempts. After an easy drill is mastered, a more difficult one should be selected. This is using progression to increase skill.

A third characteristic of good practice is a high level of concentration on technique. This attention to mental detail is vital in the attainment of good skills. A good practice should be tiring mentally as well as physically.

The old saying, "Practice makes perfect," is not really true. A more accurate statement is "Perfect practice makes perfect." The following suggestions for practice should be selected and/or modified for each player so that practice can be "tailor-made" for the individual.

Mimetic Drills

1. Practice forearm pronation and supination. Listen for the "swish" of the racket. Maintain the correct grip.
2. Practice all strokes without using a shuttle. Listen for the "swishing" sound when executing clears, smashes, long serves, and other high speed strokes. Ask your instructor or another student to check parts of the stroke for accuracy of form.

Mimetic drills

3. Move in the correct footwork patterns to the four corners of the court and hit an imaginary shot. Return to the ready position between each shot. Ask a fellow student to give commands such as net/left, net/right, back/left, back/right. Hit underhand shots at the net and overheads from the back court.

4. Use an imaginary clock face to identify areas of the court. Practice moving to the different numbers to stroke. A partner can call out the positions. Be sure to return to the ready position between each stroke.

Wall Drills

1. Use the wall to practice clears. The drill is begun by serving the shuttle to the wall with enough force to produce a good rebound. The type of shuttle used for outdoor play works well for wall rallying. Experiment by hitting all underhands or all overhands. Attempt to increase the number of consecutive hits.

2. Serves can also be practiced at the wall. Place tape on the wall at center net height of five feet and at a height of five feet, six inches. Serve from a line six to eight feet away, attempting to hit the wall between the two lines. Modify the distance between the two lines to match skill level.

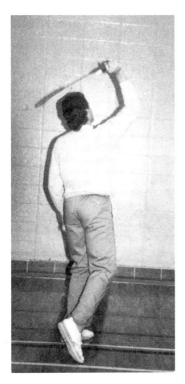

Wall drills   Partner drills

Partner Drills

1. All basic strokes with the exception of the serve can be practiced under near-game conditions by having a partner hit a set-up shot for the player to hit. The difficulty rating of this type of practice is determined by the accuracy and speed of the set-up. For beginners the set-up should be hit within easy reach of the hitter and at a moderate speed. As skill increases, more movement to reach the shuttle should be required as well as additional shuttle speed. At least ten set-ups per skill should be made before changing to a new skill or having the setter and hitter exchange roles. Clears, drop shots, smashes, drives and round-the-head shots can all be practiced in this manner. Targets for different shots can be identified; for example, back alley for clears, in front of short service line for drop shots.

2. As skill improves, partners can rally and hit continuous clears, drives, drop shots and round-the-head shots. It is very important to focus on certain strokes and to strive to hit a particular shot. Special attention should be given to all backhand strokes since there is a strong tendency to avoid them. Try to hit 10 consecutive forehand clears, 10 backhand clears, 10 forehand drives, etc.

Competitive games

3. The combining of strokes into one drill is excellent practice for more advanced players. Plan a sequence of strokes with your partner. Some examples are: serve, clear, drop, drop, clear; set-up, smash, block, clear; and serve, clear to backhand, clear go forehand, drop, clear to backhand. The sequences should be repeated until an error is made.

Competitive Games

After noncompetitive practice has increased skill, competitive games that focus on one or two skills and use small areas of the court can contribute to skill mastery.

1. A net game can be used to practice the short serve and net drops. One player serves from the regular serving position into the diagonal service court. The receiver returns with a net drop and the players continue by hitting net drops only until an error occurs. Any shot after the service that would pass the short service line is a fault.

2. The half court game uses the long serve, clears, drops and smashes. The court is divided by the middle service line and its imaginary continuation to the net. The doubles sideline is used for the other side boundary. Serves are delivered straight across instead of diagonally. Consult regular singles rules for additional procedures.

3. An advanced form of half court play uses the long serve, clears, and drop shots. To be legal all drop shots must be hit between the net and the short service line and all clears must be hit toward the back alley. This game teaches control of drops and develops power for clears. Physical conditioning is another benefit.

4. Practice a wall rally by hitting the shuttle against a wall from a distance varying from five to ten feet. As you move farther from the wall, increase the strength of your stroke. This will cause the shuttle to rebound faster, increasing your reaction time.

SUGGESTED PRACTICE DRILLS

Service Drills

1. Practice high deep serves to target areas in the backcourt.

2. Have your partner stand in the normal receiving position for singles, racket held overhead, and practice serving high and deep over your partner to the backcourt.

3. Practice short low serves to an area within 12 inches of the short service line.

4. Draw a one-foot box in each short corner of the right and left service courts. Practice serving to these areas.

5. Tie a string 8 inches above the net and practice serving the short low serve beneath the string into the target area of the doubles service court.

6. Practice until you have success in serving into your target areas with a high degree of consistency and accuracy.

7. Use partner drills to establish game conditions for serving and receiving and for varying both serves and returns.

Drive Drills

1. With a partner, practice a rapid exchange of both forehand and backhand drives. Increase the pace from slow to fast.

2. Alternate forehand and backhand drives with your partner.

3. Using a partner, practice a serve-drive return sequence.

4. Have four players in each court, and alternate hitting the shuttle to the partners on the other side. This will allow both cross-court and down-the-line drive returns.

Drop Drills

1. Stand within the short service line and practice hairpin drops with your partner, who is on the other side of the net.
2. Practice both hairpin and cross-court drops using four players at the net. Player A hits a hairpin to B, who cross-courts to C. C hits a hairpin to D, and D cross-courts back to A. Repeat the sequence several times in succession, without a miss if possible.
3. Have your partner stand close to the net, and begin a rally using an underhand clear by the net player and an overhead drop by the deep player. Practice 25 each before exchanging positions.
4. Play a "short game" inside the short service line with your partner on the other side of the net. Only drops can be used, and all shots must land within the short service line.
5. While your partner practices the low short serve for doubles, you practice the underhand drop to the close corner.

Smash Drills

1. Practice your smash with a partner giving you the short set-up. Aim your shot at a specific part of the opponent's court.
2. Use a sequence of shots to give you the opportunity to use the smash.
3. Alternate a smash-drop-smash-drive routine to practice these shots and also to use deception and disguise in your racket preparation procedures.

Clear Drills

1. Begin a rally with a high deep serve, and practice the clear — both forehand and backhand — to the opposite court. Continue the rally as long as possible.
2. Practice clears by hitting to opposite corners of the opponent's court.
3. Use a clear-drop sequence with a partner, alternating every five minutes.

Round-the-Head Drills

1. Using a partner to deliver the shuttle to your contact area, practice hitting several shuttles to various parts of the court with some degree of accuracy.
2. Have your partner feed the shuttle for the round-the-head shot to different areas of your court to allow sufficient practice time for this difficult stroke. Hit several strokes to each specific area of the opponent's court before moving to another depth or return area.

Chapter 17

Conditioning for Badminton

The ultimate test to determine if you are appropriately conditioned for badminton is taken at the end of an actual match and includes these questions:

1. Were you able to play the entire match without injury or strain to any part of the body?
2. Were you able to finish the match still stroking with the same power, mobility, and control that you possessed at the beginning of the match?
3. Would you be able to play another match with only minimal rest?

In order to answer these questions affirmatively, two types of preparation are necessary — short-term (warm-up exercises) and long-term (developmental exercises). This chapter contains suggestions for planning individual programs to cover both aspects of conditioning.

WARM-UP PROGRAMS

Although there is some reason to believe performance is enhanced by a proper warm-up, the major purpose is to prevent injury. An attempt to involve all the body parts used in badminton is essential; warm-ups must include the whole body. Another guide in designing appropriate exercises is to analyze the particular way in which the body will be used as you play a match. There will be flexibility movement — bending and stretching; agility movement — quick stops, starts, and changes of direction; and cardiorespiratory endurance movement — continuous motion with little resting time.

Flexibility Exercises

Flexibility exercises focus on joint actions and should attempt to move the joints through their fullest range of motion. During the warm-up process, however, the joints should not be extended beyond a normal comfortable range. Before beginning play you should bend and stretch all body joints. Flexibility exercises should precede other forms of warm-ups. Suggested exercises for major joints areas follow:

1. Neck: head nodding, neck rolls
2. Shoulders: arm raises to full overhead position, large and small arm circles (clockwise and counterclockwise), shoulder rotations in both directions, hang from a bar by one arm with body weight partially supported while slowly rotating the arm in both directions
3. Back: trunk twists, pull knees to chest, bend forward while seated, hang from a bar, seal raise exercises
4. Hips and thighs: seated alternate toe touches, from hands and knees position extend and raise each leg alternately, lunges
5. Ankles and lower legs: ankle rotations, raise on toes, Achilles tendon stretcher.

Agility Exercises

If the joints and connecting tissues have been thoroughly warmed up using the suggested flexibility exercises, they should be able to withstand the stress of quick starts, stops, and changes in direction required during a match. Specific exercises for agility are described below:

1. ɔlide back and forth from sideline to sideline as quickly as possible.
2. Run backwards and forwards between net and baseline using quick starts and stops.
3. Practice the mimetic footwork drill to the four corners of the court (see Chapter 14).
4. Run in place changing your speed abruptly from slow to fast.

When working on agility be sure to concentrate on keeping your body in a balanced position and moving smoothly.

Cardiorespiratory Endurance Exercises

Exercises that increase the heart rate and cause deep breathing are appropriate for this part of the warm-up. Exercises for flexibility and agility will begin this process and may be sufficient for many players. If additional warm-up is desired, exercises can be selected from these examples:

1. Running in place or laps around the play area
2. Side-straddle hops
3. Burpees
4. Stride-jumps

Combination Exercises

The best method for combination of badminton warm-up movements is to practice strokes with another player. After using the specific flexibility, agility, and cardiorespiratory exercises, gather your equipment and another player and begin rallying over the net. Start by hitting easily and with accuracy to the other player, then gradually increase force and begin to hit to all areas of the court. Combinations of clears and drop shots are good warm-ups requiring flexibility, agility, and cardiorespiratory endurance.

The optimum time to spend on warm-up exercises will vary from individual to individual. Trust your feelings to guide you. Warm-ups should be refreshing rather than tiring. Try spending approximately 10 to 15 minutes for each specific exercise and the badminton-related activity to see how your body reacts.

Knees to chest

Neck rolls

Sit-ups

Lunge

Hamstring stretch

Alternate seated toe touch

Leg press

Leg press

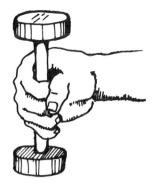

Wrist pronation

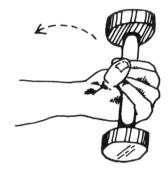

Wrist flexion

Wrist supination

Hip rotator

DEVELOPMENTAL PROGRAMS

The purpose of a developmental conditioning program for badminton is to improve the physiological qualities necessary to play a vigorous match with no loss of power, mobility, or control from beginning to end. This requires a long-term conditioning program. The competitive tournament player uses a developmental program in the off-season. The student in a beginning badminton class could benefit from utilizing a developmental program, alternating days with the skill development class.

The physiological qualities that need developing are basically the same as those emphasized in the warm-up program: flexibility, agility, cardiorespiratory endurance and increased muscular strength and endurance. The developmental program should focus on overload, working beyond the comfort range both in intensity and duration of the workouts.

Flexibility

Use the same flexibility exercises suggested for warm-up programs, increasing the repetitions and attempting slowly to increase the range of motion in each joint. Static stretching is preferred to a jerky or bouncing movement. Be sure to increase gradually your stretching and bending to avoid soreness and discomfort.

Agility

Because of its vital role in footwork, agility should not be neglected in your developmental program. Some players seem to have "quick feet" naturally but most must develop this quality. Drills that include arm and hand movement with quick starts and stops add a further dimension. Some suggestions for combined drills follow:

1. Running lines: Using any type of court or field with multiple lines, begin at one sideline and run to the first line, touch it with your hand and run back to the sideline, touch it and run back past line one and touch the next line. Continue the process until all lines have been touched.

2. Shuttle run: Sprint back and forth between two lines, transporting objects from one line to the other. Shuttlecocks can be used. Another variation is to touch the lines with your racket as you travel back and forth. Sidelines of a badminton court can be used.

3. Since badminton play requires unexpected changes of direction, have an assistant give commands for moving to various areas on the court to hit an imaginary shuttle. Return to ready position at midcourt after each command is executed. Use proper footwork patterns.

Cardiorespiratory Endurance

This is the quality that can be improved only in the developmental phase since warm-up programs do not provide sufficient time to develop endurance. Workouts of at least 20 to 30 minutes three or four times a week are recommended for increasing cardiorespiratory endurance. Exercise must be intense enough to increase heart rate and breathing appropriate to your recommended "target zone." Once the "target zone" is reached, it must be maintained for at least 15 to 20 minutes. Use the overload principle and begin your program with short periods of work and gradually lengthen the time until you are at the 20 to 30 minute range. Suggested activities include jogging, rope jumping, swimming, biking, and brisk walking.

To make this part of your conditioning program relate more closely to actual game conditions, vary your speed as you work. For example, when jogging, intersperse brief sprints of five yards periodically, and occasionally jog backwards or laterally as you run.

Muscular Strength and Endurance

Because of the light-weight equipment used in badminton, great amounts of muscular strength and endurance are unnecessary. However, an analysis of the requirements of play indicates muscular needs in two specific areas: legs and racket arm. Leg strength is involved in the power used to make quick starts and stops. Endurance is needed for the constant sprinting from area to area on the court. Arm strength and endurance are necessary to produce the pronation and supination of the forearm, vital for most strokes. Giving attention to these two areas in the design of your developmental program may give you a competitive edge over your favorite opponent. Emphasize endurance in this phase of your program by increasing repetitions rather than increasing the intensity of the work done. Suggestions of appropriate exercises follow:

1. Legs: Stride jumps, side-straddle hop, jump and click heels, leg presses with light weights.

2. Arms: Using a light weight (one to three pounds), do wrist flexion/extension exercises and forearm pronation/supination exercises.

Combination Exercises

As in the warm-up phase, good developmental conditioning can occur on the court while playing or rallying with another player. For development this activity must be longer and more vigorous than for the warm-up. Choose a player of equal ability and you'll be assured of long rallies that can enhance your endurance. Hitting continuous clears from one baseline to the other is an excellent means for developing muscular endurance of the racket arm. Alternate clears and drop shots will build cardiorespiratory endurance and agility.

Participation in other sports and activities can also build or maintain the physiological qualities needed for good badminton performance. Soccer, basketball, squash, tennis, handball, racketball, and dance are examples.

Tips for Conditioning

1. Always warm up before a match by using specific exercises and related badminton activities.

2. Individualize your warm-up and developmental program based on your personal needs as a badminton player. Highly competitive tournament players have greater needs than recreational players. Set realistic goals.

3. Use the principle of overload in designing your program; gradually increase the work until you meet your goals.

4. When using skill-related activities for conditioning, practice correct techniques and footwork.

Name_____

Chapter 17 Evaluation

1. Distinguish between the purposes of warm-up exercise programs and developmental programs.

2. What physiological qualities are included in a warm-up program? A developmental program?

3. What are your realistic goals as a badminton player? What should you include in a developmental program to meet those goals?

4. What exercises would you include to warm up for an important match?

(Over)

5. Name two exercises or activities for each quality below:

   a. Flexibility:

   b. Cardiorespiratory Endurance:

   c. Agility:

   d. Muscular Endurance and Strength
      Arms:

      Legs:

6. How is the overload principle used to develop physiological qualities?

Chapter 18

Laws of Badminton

(Reprinted with permission of the International Badminton Federation, 24 Winchcombe House, Winchcombe Street, Cheltenham, Gloucestershire, England.)

THE LAWS OF BADMINTON
AS REVISED IN THE YEAR 1939
and adopted by
THE INTERNATIONAL BADMINTON FEDERATION.
(Incorporating all amendments subsequently adopted).

*Note: Imperial measurements, some of which vary slightly from the metric measurements, are quoted in brackets and comply with the Laws.

COURT

1. (a) The court shall be laid out as in the following diagram "A" (except in the case provided for in paragraph (b) of this Law) and to the measurements there shown, and shall be defined preferably by white or yellow lines, or, if this is not possible, by other easily distinguishable lines, 40 mm. (1½ inches) wide.

In marking the court, the width 40 mm. (1½ inches) of the centre lines shall be equally divided between the right and left service courts; the width 40 mm. each (1½ inches each) of the short service line and the long service line shall fall within the 3.96 metres (13 feet) measurement given as the length of the service court; and the width 40 mm. each (1½ inches each) of all other boundary lines shall fall within the measurements given.

(b) Where space does not permit of the marking out of a court for doubles, a court may be marked out for singles only as shown in diagram "B". The back boundary lines become also the long service lines, and the posts, or the strips of materials representing them as referred to in Law 2, shall be placed on the side lines.

POSTS

2. The posts shall be 1.55 metres (5 feet 1 inch) in height from the surface of the court. They shall be sufficiently firm to keep the net strained as provided in Law 3, and shall be placed on the side boundary lines of the court. Where this is not practicable, some method must be employed for indicating the position of the side boundary line where it passes under the net, e.g., by the use of a thin post or strips of material, not less than 40 mm. (1½ inches) in width, fixed to the side boundary line and rising vertically to the net cord. Where this is in use on a court marked for doubles it shall be placed on the side boundary line of the doubles court irrespective of whether singles or doubles are being played.

NET

3. The net shall be made of fine natural cord or artificial fibre of a dark colour and an even thickness not less than 15 mm. (⅝ inch) and not more than 20 mm. (¾ inch) mesh. It shall be firmly stretched from post to post, and shall be 760 mm. (2 feet 6 inches) in depth. The top of the net shall be 1.524 metres (5 feet) in height from the floor at the centre, and 1.55 metres (5 feet 1 inch) at the posts, and shall be edged with a 75 mm. (3 inches) white tape doubled and supported by a cord or cable run through the tape and strained over and flush with the top of the posts.

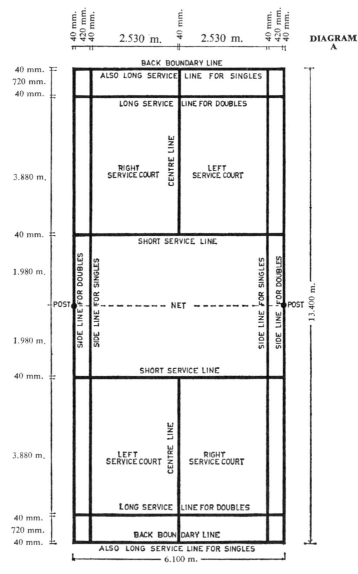

DIAGRAM A

Note: Court which can be used for both singles and doubles play.

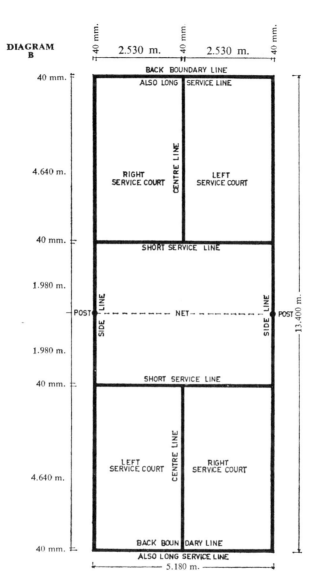

DIAGRAM B

40 mm.

2.530 m.

40 mm.

2.530 m.

40 mm.

40 mm.

BACK BOUNDARY LINE

ALSO LONG SERVICE LINE

4.640 m.

RIGHT SERVICE COURT

CENTRE LINE

LEFT SERVICE COURT

40 mm.

SHORT SERVICE LINE

1.980 m.

POST

SIDE LINE

NET

SIDE LINE

POST

13.400 m.

1.980 m.

40 mm.

SHORT SERVICE LINE

LEFT SERVICE COURT

CENTRE LINE

RIGHT SERVICE COURT

4.640 m.

BACK BOUNDARY LINE

40 mm.

ALSO LONG SERVICE LINE

5.180 m.

Note: Court which can only be used for singles play.

SHUTTLE

4. (a) (i) **General Design**

A shuttle shall have 14 to 16 feathers fixed in a cork base which is 25 mm. to 28 mm. (1 inch to 1⅛ inches) in diameter. The feathers shall be from 64 mm. to 70 mm. (2½ to 2¾ inches) in length from the tip to the top of the cork base.

The tips of the feathers shall form a circle with a diameter within the range of 54 mm. to 64 mm. (2⅛ to 2½ inches). The feathers shall be fastened firmly with thread or other suitable material.

The bottom of the cork shall be rounded and covered by a thin layer of white leather or a material with similar properties.

4. (a) (ii)   **Synthetic Shuttles**
A skirt of synthetic material replaces the natural feathers. The base shall be of cork covered with a thin layer of white leather or a material with similar properties. Alternatively, the base can be made of synthetic material having similar properties and feel on the racket strings as cork covered by a thin layer of leather. The bottom of the base shall be rounded.
The flight characteristics shall be similar to those of a feathered shuttle.
Measurements shall be the same as in paragraph 4 (a) (i). However, because of the differences in the specific gravity and behaviour of synthetic materials in comparison with feathers, a variation of up to 10% in the measurements stated is acceptable.

(b) **Weight**
A shuttle shall weigh from 4.74 to 5.50 grammes (73 to 85 grains).

(c) **Pace and Flight**
A shuttle shall be deemed to be of correct pace when it is hit by a player with a full underhand stroke from a spot immediately above one back boundary line in a direction parallel to the side lines and at an upward angle, to fall not less than 300 mm. (one foot) and not more than 760 mm. (two feet six inches) short of the other back boundary line.

(d) Subject to there being no variation in the general design, weight, pace and flight of the shuttle, modifications in the above specifications may be made, with the approval of the national organization concerned:

i) in places where atmospheric conditions due either to altitude or climate make the standard shuttle unsuitable; or

ii) if special circumstances exist which make it otherwise necessary in the interests of the game.

PLAYERS

5. (a) The word "Player" applies to all those taking part in a game.

(b) The game shall be played, in the case of the doubles game, by two players a side, and in the case of the singles game, by one player a side.

(c) The side for the time being having the right to serve shall be called the "In" side, and the opposing side shall be called the "Out" side.

THE TOSS

6. Before commencing play the opposing sides shall toss, and the side winning the toss shall have the option of: —
(a) Serving first ; or
(b) Not serving first ; or
(c) Choosing ends.
The side losing the toss shall then have choice of any alternative remaining.

SCORING

7. (a) The doubles and men's singles game consists of 15 points provided that, when the score is 13-all, the side which first reached 13 has the option of "setting" the game to 5, and that when the score is 14-all, the side which first reached 14 has the option of 'setting' the game to 3. After a game has been 'set' the score is called 'love all', and the side which first scores 5 or 3 points, according as the game has been 'set' at 13 all or 14 all, wins the game. In either case the claim to 'set' the game must be made before the next service is delivered after the score has reached 13 all or 14 all.

(b) The ladies' singles game consists of 11 points. Provided that when the score is "9 all" the player who first reached 9 has the option of "setting" the game to 3, and when the score is "10 all" the player who first reached 10 has the option of "setting" the game to 2.

(c) A side rejecting the option of "setting" at the first opportunity shall not thereby be debarred from "setting" if a second opportunity arises.

(d) Notwithstanding paragraph (a) above, it is permissible by prior arrangement for only one game to be played and also for this to consist of 21 points, in which case "setting" shall be as for the game of 15 points with scores of 19 and 20 being substituted for 13 and 14 respectively.

(e) In handicap games "setting" is not permitted.

8. The opposing sides shall contest the best of three games, unless otherwise agreed. The players shall change ends at the commencement of the second game and also of the third game (if any). In the third game the players shall change ends when the leading score reaches: —

   (a) 8 in a game of 15 points ;
   (b) 6 in a game of 11 points ;

   or, in handicap events, when one of the sides has scored half the total number of points required to win the game (the next highest number being taken in case of fractions). When it has been agreed to play only one game the players shall change ends as provided above for the third game. In a game of 21 points, the players shall change ends when the leading score reaches 11 or in handicap games as indicated above.

   If, inadvertently, the players omit to change ends as provided in this Law at the score indicated, the ends shall be changed immediately the mistake is discovered, and the existing score shall stand.

DOUBLES PLAY

9. (a) It having been decided which side is to have the first service, the player in the right-hand service court of that side commences the game by serving to the player in the service court diagonally opposite. If the latter player returns the shuttle before it touches the ground, it is to be returned by one of the "In" side, then returned by one of the "Out" side, and so on, till a fault is made or the shuttle ceases to be "in play" (vide paragraph (b)). If a fault is made by the "In" side its right to continue serving is lost, as only one player on the side beginning a game is entitled to do so (vide Law 11), and the opponent in the right-hand service court then becomes the server; but if the service is not returned, or the fault is made by the "Out" side, the "In" side scores a point. The "In" side players then change from one service court to the other, the service now being from the left-hand service court to the player in the service court diagonally opposite. So long as a side remains "in", service is delivered alternately from each service court into the one diagonally opposite, the change being made by the "In" side when, and only when, a point is added to its score.

   (b) The first service of a side in each innings shall be made from the right-hand service court. A "Service" is delivered as soon as the shuttle is struck by the server's racket. The shuttle is thereafter "in play" until it touches the ground, or until a fault or "let" occurs. or except as provided in Law 19. After the service is delivered the server and the player served to may take up any positions they choose on their side of the net, irrespective of any boundary lines.

10. The player served to may alone receive the service, but should the shuttle touch, or be struck by, his partner the "In" side scores a point. No player may receive two consecutive services in the same game, except as provided in Law 12.

11. Only one player of the side beginning a game shall be entitled to serve in its first innings. In all subsequent innings each partner shall have the right, and they shall serve consecutively. The side winning a game shall always serve first in the next game, but either of the winners may serve and either of the losers may receive the service.

12. If a player serves out of turn, or from the wrong service court (owing to a mistake as to the service court from which service is at the time being in order), *and his side wins the rally,* it shall be a "Let", provided that such "Let" be claimed and allowed, or ordered by the umpire, before the next succeeding service is delivered.

If a player of the "Out" side standing in the wrong service court is prepared to receive the service when it is delivered, *and his side wins the rally,* it shall be a "Let", provided that such "Let" be claimed and allowed, or ordered by the umpire, before the next succeeding service is delivered.

If in either of the above cases the side at fault *loses the rally,* the mistake shall stand and the players' positions shall not be corrected.

Should a player inadvertently change sides when he should not do so, and the mistake not be discovered until after the next succeeding service has been delivered, the mistake shall stand, and a "Let" cannot be claimed or allowed, and the players' position shall not be corrected.

SINGLES PLAY

13. In singles Laws 9 to 12 hold good except that:—

(a) The players shall serve from and receive service in their respective right-hand service courts only when the server's score is 0 or an even number of points in the game, the service being delivered from and received in their respective left-hand service courts when the server's score is an odd number of points. Setting does not affect this sequence.

(b) Both players shall change service courts after each point has been scored.

FAULTS

14. A fault made by a player of the side which is "In", puts the server out; if made by a player whose side is "Out", it counts a point to the "In" side.

It is a fault:—

(a) If in serving, (i) the initial point of contact with the shuttle is not on the base of the shuttle, or (ii) any part of the shuttle at the instant of being struck be higher than the server's waist, or (iii) if at the instant of the shuttle being struck the shaft of the racket be not pointing in a downward direction to such an extent that the whole of the head of the racket is discernibly below the whole of the server's hand holding the racket.

(b) If, in serving, the shuttle does not pass over the net, or falls into the wrong service court (*i.e.,* into the one not diagonally opposite to the server), or falls short of the short service line or beyond the long service line, or outside the side boundary lines of the service court into which service is in order.

(c) If the server's feet are not in the service court from which service is at the time being in order, or if the feet of the player receiving the service are not in the service court diagonally opposite until the service is delivered. (Vide Law 16).

(d) If, once the service has started, any player makes preliminary feints or otherwise intentionally baulks his opponent, or if any player deliberately delays serving the shuttle or in getting ready to receive it so as to obtain an unfair advantage. (When the server and receiver have taken up their respective positions to serve and to receive, the first forward movement of the server's racket constitutes the start of the service and such must be continuous thereafter.)

(e) If, either in service or play, the shuttle falls outside the boundaries of the court, or passes through or under the net, or fails to pass the net, or touches the roof or side walls, or the person or dress of a player. (A shuttle falling on a line shall be deemed to have fallen in the court or service court of which such line is a boundary).

(f) If, when in play, the initial point of contact with the shuttle is not on the striker's side of the net. (The striker may, however, follow the shuttle over the net with his racket in the course of stroke.)

(g) If, when the shuttle is "in play", a player touches the net or its supports with racket, person or dress.

(h) If the shuttle be caught and held on the racket and then slung during the execution of a stroke; or if the shuttle be hit twice in succession by the same player with two strokes; or if the shuttle be hit by a player and his partner successively.

(i) If, in play, a player strikes the shuttle (unless he thereby makes a good return) or is struck by it, whether he is standing within or outside the boundaries of the court.

(j) If a player obstructs an opponent.

(k) If Law 16 be transgresssed.

(l) If a player is guilty of flagrant or persistent misconduct under Law 21.

GENERAL

15. The server may not serve till his opponent is ready, but the opponent shall be deemed to be ready if a return of the service be attempted.

16. The server and the player served to must stand within the limits of their respective service courts (as bounded by the short and long service, the centre, and side lines), and some part of both feet of these players must remain in contact with the surface of the court in a stationary position until the service is delivered. A foot on or touching a line in the case of either the server or the receiver shall be held to be outside his service court (vide Law 14 (c)). The respective partners may take up any position, provided they do not unsight or otherwise obstruct an opponent.

17. (a) If, in the course of service or rally, the shuttle touches and passes over the net, the stroke is not invalidated thereby. It is a good return if the shuttle having passed outside either post drops on or within the boundary lines of the opposite court. A "Let" may be given by the umpire for any unforeseen or accidental hindrance.

(b) If, in service, or during a rally, a shuttle, *after passing over the net,* is caught in or on the net, it is a "Let."

(c) If the receiver is faulted for moving before the service is delivered, or for not being within the correct service court, in accordance with Laws 14 (c) or 16, and at the same time the server is also faulted for a service infringement, it shall be a let.

(d) When a "Let" occurs, the play since the last service shall not count, and the player who served shall serve again, except when Law 12 is applicable.

18. If the server, in attempting to serve, misses the shuttle, it is not a fault; but if the shuttle be touched by the racket, a service is thereby delivered.

19. If, when in play, the shuttle strikes the net and remains suspended there, or strikes the net and falls towards the surface of the court on the striker's side of the net, or hits the surface outside the court and an opponent then touches the net or shuttle with his racket or person, there is no penalty, as the shuttle is not *then* in play.

20. If a player has a chance of striking the shuttle in a downward direction when quite near the net, his opponent must not put up his racket near the net on the chance of the shuttle rebounding from it. This is obstruction within the meaning of Law 14 (j).

A player may, however, hold up his racket to protect his face from being hit if he does not thereby baulk his opporent.

21. If a player deliberately interferes with the speed of a shuttle or behaves in an offensive manner or is guilty of misconduct not otherwise covered by the Laws of Badminton, the umpire shall:
(a) issue a warning to the player and
(b) fault the offender in flagrant or persistent cases.
If, after the umpire has taken action under (b) above, the player continues to offend under Law 21 the umpire may report the offence to the referee and the referee shall have the power to disqualify the offending side.

22. It shall be the duty of the umpire to call "fault" or "let" should either occur, without appeal being made by the players, and to give his decision on any appeal regarding a point in dispute, if made before the next service; and also to appoint linesmen and service judges at his discretion. The umpire's decision shall be final, but he shall uphold the decision of a linesman or service judge. This shall not preclude the umpire also from faulting the server or receiver. Where, however, a referee is appointed, an appeal shall lie to him from the decision of an umpire on questions of law only.

Continuous Play

23. (a) Play shall be continuous from the first service until the match be concluded; except that:-

(i) in international competitive events there shall be allowed an interval not exceeding five minutes between the second and third games of a match;

(ii) in countries where conditions render it desirable, there shall be allowed, subject to the previously published approval of the national organization concerned, an interval not exceeding five minutes between the second and third games of a match, either singles or doubles or both;

(iii) when necessitated by circumstances not within the control of the players, the umpire may suspend play for such a period as he may consider necessary. If play be suspended the existing score shall stand and play be resumed from that point.

(b) Under no circumstances shall play be suspended to enable a player to recover his strength or wind, or to receive instruction or advice.

(c) Except that in the case of an interval provided for above, without the umpire's consent no player shall be allowed to receive advice during a match or to leave the court until the match be concluded.

(d) The umpire shall be the sole judge of any suspension of play and he shall have the right to disqualify an offender.

NOTE

INTERVALS IN PLAY AS SANCTIONED BY THE I.B.F.

The international competitive events referred to in (a) (i) above are :
(1) *The Thomas Cup and Uber Cup;*
(2) *The World Championships ;*
(3) *All official international matches ;*
(4) *International Open Championships and other international events of a higher status as sanctioned by the I.B.F.*

INTERPRETATIONS.

1. Any movement or conduct by the server that has the effect of breaking the continuity of service after the server and receiver have taken their position to serve and to receive the service is a preliminary feint. For example, a server who, after having taken up his position to serve, delays hitting the shuttle for so long as to be unfair to the receiver, is guilty of such conduct.
(Vide Law 14 (d)).

2. It is obstruction if a player invades an opponent's court with racket or person in any degree except as permitted in Law 14 (f).
(Vide Law 14 (j)).

3. Where necessary on account of the structure of a building, the local Badminton authority may, subject to the right of veto of its national organisation, make bye-laws dealing with cases in which a shuttle touches an obstruction.

RECOMMENDATIONS TO UMPIRES

ADOPTED, 1960.

(incorporating all amendments subsequently adopted)

1. Thoroughly know "The Laws of Badminton."

2. The umpire's decision is final on all points of fact: a player may, however, appeal to the referee on a point of Law only.

3. The linesman's decision is final on all points of fact on his own line: the umpire cannot overrule him. If a linesman is unsighted, the umpire may then give a decision if he can: otherwise a let should be played.

4. Where a service judge is appointed, his decision is final on all points of fact in connection with the delivery of the service as set out in "Service Judge" 27. It shall be the duty of the umpire specially to watch the receiver —see 22 (c).

5. All announcements and calling of the score must be done distinctly and loudly enough to be heard clearly by players and spectators.

Call promptly and with authority but, if a mistake is made, admit it, apologise and correct it.

6. If a decision cannot be given, say so and give a let. NEVER ask spectators nor be influenced by their remarks.

7. The umpire is responsible for all lines not covered by linesmen.

8. The umpire should control the match firmly, but without being officious. He should keep play flowing without unnecessary interruptions while ensuring that the Laws are observed. The game is for the players.

9. When a doubt arises in the mind of the umpire or service judge as to whether an infringement of the Laws has occurred or not, "Fault" should not be called and the game allowed to proceed.

Before Play Begins

10. Obtain the score pad from the referee. Enter up the score pad.

11. Check the net for height. See that the posts are on the lines, or that tapes are correctly placed—Laws 2 and 3.

12. Ensure that the linesmen and service judge are correctly placed and know their job—see "Linesmen" and "Service Judge."

13. Ensure that a sufficient quantity of tested shuttles according to Law 4 is readily available for the match, in order to avoid delays during play. If the players cannot agree, the umpire should have the shuttles tested, or in a tournament refer to the referee, or in a match the captains or referee. Once shuttles have been found to be acceptable, ensure that they are used unless circumstances alter.

Starting the Match

14. Ensure that tossing is correctly carried out, and that the winners and losers exercise correctly their options under Law 6.

15. In the case of doubles, mark on the score pad the names of the players starting in the right-hand service courts. This enables a check to be made at any time to see if the players are in their correct service courts. If during the game the players get in their wrong service courts unnoticed, so that they have to stay wrong—Law 12—amend the score pad accordingly.

16. When the players have finished warming-up, announce:—

    (a) In a tournament:—

        1. "Final or semi-final of . . . . " If neither, say nothing

    (b) In a tournament or match:—

        1. Names of players with country, county or club where applicable.

        2. Name of the first server, and, in the case of doubles, of the receiver.

        3. To start a match, call "Love all, play."

The Match

17. Mark the score pad as the match proceeds.

18. Call the score:—

    (a) Always call the server's score first.

    (b) Singles—when a player loses his service, call "Service over" followed by the score in favour of the new server.

    (c) Doubles—at the beginning of a game call the score only, and continue to do so as long as the first player serves. When the right to serve is lost call "Service over" followed by the score in favour of the new server. In that and subsequent innings when the first server loses his right to serve, call the score followed by "Second server." Continue this as long as the second player serves. When a side loses the right to serve call "Service over" followed by the score in favour of the new server.

    (d) When a side reaches 14, or in the case of ladies' singles 10, call on the first occasion only "Game point" or "Match point." If a further game or match point occurs after setting, call it again on the first occasion. "Game point" or "Match point" should always immediately follow the server's score where applicable, and precede the receiver's score.

(e) When the shuttle falls outside a line for which the umpire is responsible in the absence of a linesman, call "Out" before calling the score.

19. See that no unnecessary delay occurs, or that the players do not leave the court without the permission of the umpire—Law 22.

20. If an unavoidable hold-up occurs in a match, record the score, server and the correct service courts of the players on the score pad.

21. If a shuttle or other object not connected with the match in progress invades the court or its environs, "Let" should be called.

22. Look for:—

(a) Faulty serving if there is no service judge. It is difficult to detect from the chair "Serving above the waist", or "racket head above the hand." If there is any doubt, caution the player and ask for a service judge.

(b) The server having both feet on the surface of the court in a stationary position INSIDE the service court when the shuttle is struck, and that there is no feint—Law 14(d) and Interpretation 1. This should be the responsibility of the service judge if available. Where the official responsible considers that there has been a flagrant fault under Law 14(d), as described in Interpretation 1, he shall fault the server as soon as the service is delivered. However, each case should be judged on its merits and, if it is considered that the server tends to delay too long, the umpire should, either on his responsibility, or at the request of the service judge, warn the player that he will be faulted should he continue to delay. (See also Recommendation 33).

(c) The receiver having both feet on the surface of the court in a stationary position INSIDE the service court until the service is delivered, and that he does not move before the shuttle is struck—Laws 14(c) and 16.

(d) Strokes which are faults under Law 14(h). These should be immediately called by the umpire as "Fault".

(e) Do not permit players to call 'no shot,' 'fault,' etc. Warn them if they do, as it may distract their opponents.

(f) Obstruction: for example, sliding under the net; throwing the racket into the opponent's court; baulking; unsighting an opponent during service. See Laws 14(d), 14(j), 16, 20 and Interpretation 2.

(g) Serving and receiving out of turn or in the wrong court. Law 12 should be thoroughly understood.

(h) Striking the shuttle before it crosses the net, and hitting the net with racket, person or dress, while the shuttle is in play—Laws 14(f) and 14(g).

(i) The option of "setting" being correctly exercised—Law 7. It is the duty of the umpire to ask the player's or players' decision. Announce the decision loudly so that spectators can hear, calling "Set 2 points" (or 3 or 5 as appropriate) followed by "Love all" or "Love all, second server," as the case may be.

(j) The players changing ends at the correct score in the third game Law 8.

(k) A player interfering with the correct speed of a shuttle. The player should be warned, and the shuttle discarded if necessary.

The End of a Game

23. Announce:—"Game to . . . . " (the name(s) of the player(s) in a tournament or the name of the team represented in the case of a meeting of representative teams) followed by the score and, if appropriate, by "One game all".

In the case of a match in a meeting between two teams, always define the contestants by the name of the team represented and not by the names of the actual players.

The End of the match

24. Announce the result and score.

25. Immediately take the completed and signed score pad to the referee in a tournament, or to the captains in a match.

Service judge

*26. The service judge should sit on a low chair by the net post preferably opposite the umpire, but on the same side as the umpire if circumstances so dictate.

*27. The service judge is responsible for seeing that the server:—

(a) until the shuttle is struck, has some part of both feet in a stationary position on the surface of the court INSIDE the service court—Law 16 and Recommendation 32—and does not feint—Law 14(d) and Interpretation 1.

(b) at the moment of striking the shuttle does not have ANY part of the racket above ANY part of the hand holding the racket—Law 14(a) (see diagram) and does not have any part of the shuttle above his waist— Law 14(a).

*28. If the server does not comply with all of 27 the service judge should immediately call "Fault" loudly and ensure that the umpire hears him. In addition this shall not preclude the umpire also from faulting the server.

The umpire may arrange with the service judge any extra duties which he wishes him to undertake, provided that the players are so advised.

Linesmen

*29. A linesman is entirely responsible for his line. If the shuttle falls out, no matter how far, call "Out" promptly in a clear voice loud enough to be heard by the players and the spectators, and at the same time signal by extending both arms horizontally so that the umpire can see clearly. If the shuttle falls in, the linesman shall say nothing, but point to the line with his right hand. If unsighted, he shall inform the umpire immediately by putting both hands up crossed to cover his eyes.

30. Linesmen should be sited on chairs in prolongation of their lines, at the ends of the court and at the side opposite to the umpire.

31. If three linesmen are available, two should take a back boundary line and (in doubles) long service line each, the third the sideline furthest from the umpire.

If further linesmen are available, they should be used according to the umpire's preference.

LAW 14—DELIVERY OF SERVICE

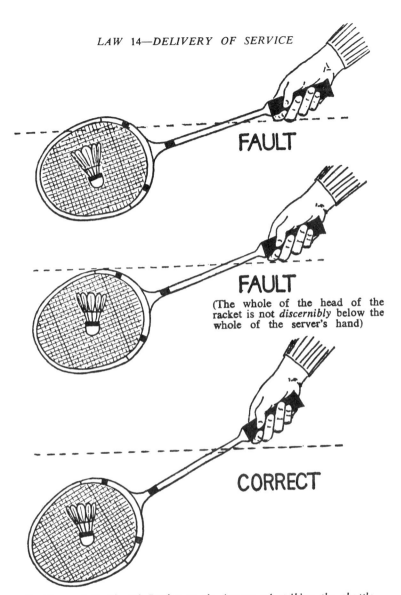

FAULT

FAULT

(The whole of the head of the racket is not *discernibly* below the whole of the server's hand)

CORRECT

Positions of Hand and Racket at the instant of striking the shuttle.

Interpretations

32. It is not a fault under Law 16 if either the server or the receiver raises any part of either or both feet, provided that some part of both feet does maintain contact with the same part of the surface of the court.

33. It is not a fault under Law 16 if the server, after having taken up his position to serve, should then take one step forward before striking the shuttle, always provided that he had not started to swing his racket forward before taking such step.

Appendix

BADMINTON SKILL TEST

Test One: Short Service

Serve ten short doubles serves into the area marked on the court (5-3-1).
Serves must go between the cord (12″) and the net.

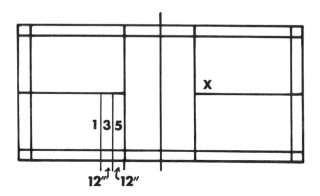

Test Two: Long Service

Serve ten long (singles) serves. Serve must fall vertically into the scoring
area marked on the court (5-3-1). Serve must go over the high cord above
the net.

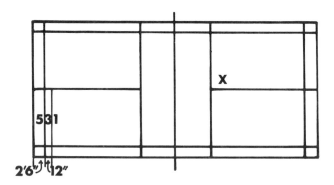

Test Three: High Clear

Hit five forehand and five backhand clears that fall vertically into the area marked for singles. Instructor or assistant will set up the shots.

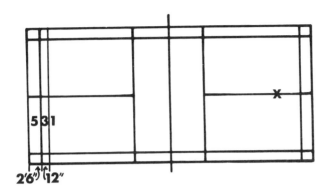

Test Four: Overhead Smash

Hit ten shots from a set up with rapid speed and a sharp angle. Hit from center court. Score five points for a good shot, zero points for a shot that is not good due to hitting in net, wood shot, slow speed, etc.

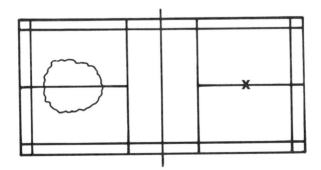

Test Five: Overhead Drop Shot
Shuttle is set up as for a smash. Execute the overhead drop shot. Shuttle must land in the area between net and short service line. Score five or zero as in test four.

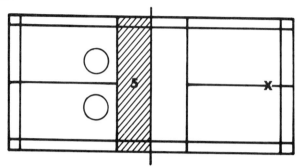

Test Six: Wall Rebound Test
Replay shuttle from wall. Thirty seconds test score one point each time the shuttle is hit to the wall. Play rebound for continuous scoring. If a miss or control is lost, continue score on next shot.

Have player stand from six to ten feet from the wall, depending on player's strength.

Test Seven: Shuttle Run
Starting at the #1 mark on the singles court, the player moves as rapidly as possible through the marked course, completing it three times under timed conditions. Two trials are given, with the best counting as the score on the skill test.

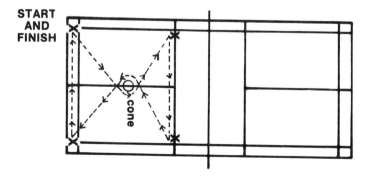

BADMINTON TEST

PART I: TRUE AND FALSE. Place a T in the answer space if the statement is true, and an F if the statement is false.

_____ 1. The major purpose of the warm-up is to prevent injury.

_____ 2. A push return directly at the server has a high degree of certainty in winning the point.

_____ 3. Short serves that are six to ten inches over the net should be immediately attacked.

_____ 4. When you sense that your opponent will charge your service, a flick service will quickly put him/her on the defensive.

_____ 5. The basic service in doubles is the driven service.

_____ 6. In singles, the high deep service is preferable to the short, low service.

_____ 7. Side-by-side formations are excellent to use when on the attack.

_____ 8. The up-and-back formation is more effective in defense against the attack than in mounting the offensive.

_____ 9. The up-and-back formation leaves the sidelines open for attack.

_____10. Since badminton is a skill game, it is more important to select a skilled partner than one who is compatible.

_____11. Disguise your stroke whenever possible to keep your opponent guessing.

_____12. Bisecting the angle of return means to stand in the center of the angle formed by the short service line and the center line.

_____13. If you are losing the contest, change your style of play.

_____14. The best return of a smash is to use either a drop shot or a clear.

_____15. Aim your high deep serve as far back in the forehand corner of the receiver's court as possible.

_____16. Defensive players win by causing the opponent to make errors.

_____17. Go into the contest with some type of game plan in mind and stick to it until it proves faulty.

_____18. The basic strategy for defensive play will be the drop-clear strategy.

_____19. Deception does not play a major part in the strategy of badminton.

_____20. The length of the badminton court is 46 feet from back line to back line.

_____21. The team on the attack will keep driving the shuttle up and away from the opponents at all cost.

_____22. Driving the shuttle at the opponents will force errors and cause mistakes to be made.

_____23. Keep the shuttle in play at all cost. This will cause the opponent to tire more quickly and begin to make numerous errors. Therefore, try not to put the point away quickly.

_____24. Driven serves should be made to the backhand corner of the opponent's receiving court.

_____25. Your enjoyment of the game of badminton will largely depend on your skill level.

_____26. Due to the small area of the court, physical conditioning is of little importance to the average player.

_____27. The two most important elements in the game are skill and physical conditioning.

_____28. The round-the-head shot is made above the left shoulder of a right-handed player.

_____29. The wrist should not be used in the round-the-head stroke.

_____30. The most vulnerable part of the body is the right should of a right-handed player.

_____31. The backhand smash is most effective when made from a position about halfway back in the service court.

_____32. The backhand grip is used for the backhand smash.

_____33. The smash should always be aimed at the opponent, for this will not allow him/her to react in time to make a safe return.

_____34. The smash should be hit with a closed racket face.

_____35. The basic purpose of the smash is to win the point outright.

_____36. Aiming the elbow at the clear will aid you in making a proper stroke sequence.

_____37. The clear should be contacted in front of the body to be most effective.

_____38. Deception should not be attempted in executing the overhead clear.

_____39. Most clears should be aimed at the backhand corner of the opponent's court.

_____40. The trajectories of the basic singles serve and the underhand clear are almost identical.

_____41. The clear is always a defensive stroke, as it has a low to high trajectory.

_____42. In singles, the clear is frequently used as much as 60 percent of the time as an effective strategy maneuver.

_____43. Both the hairpin drop and the cross-court drop should be taken as soon as the shuttle comes over the net, not allowing the shuttle to drop downward on your side.

_____44. As you plan to hit the overhead drop, think disguise.

_____45. The basic return for a smash is a drop or a clear.

_____46. Shortening the grip is permitted for the hairpin drop return.

_____47. The wrist does not come into play when serving the shuttle.

_____48. The service is basically a defensive stroke.

_____49. Drive serves are used with a high degree of frequency in both singles and doubles, and are effective in keeping the opponent off-balance.

_____50. The flick serve is best used when the server anticipates that the receiver will attack the net for a push return.

_____51. The name "poona" was another name for badminton.

_____52. A shot that hits the frame of the racket is considered a poor shot, but a legal one.

_____53. The Thomas Cup and the Uber Cup are held annually in the United States and in England, respectively.

_____54. The American Badminton Association is the governing body for badminton in the country today.

_____55. The rules of badminton have changed greatly since the game came to the United States.

_____56. The Chinese played a badminton-like game as early as 3000 years ago.

_____57. The formal name of badminton came from India.

_____58. Although badminton is not mentally challenging, the game is certainly physically taxing.

_____59. Aerobic benefits in badminton are greater than those in tennis.

_____60. The drop shot usually disguised as a smash is the hairpin drop.

_____61. In most strokes, the player should contact the shuttle as soon as possible after it crosses the net.

_____62. If the shuttle contacts the player, or his/her clothing, a let is called and the point is replayed.

_____63. When the shuttle contacts a permanent object in the area surrounding the court, the point is replayed.

_____64. The player may reach over the net in attempting to stroke the shuttle so long as he/she does not interfere with the opponent.

_____65. If the player swings but misses the shuttle while attempting to serve, he/she may repeat the attempt.

_____66. Games may only be set to either two points, or five points, and then only by the player reaching that score first.

_____67. Shuttles which land on the line are considered in bounds.

_____68. A service made into the wrong service court that is returned by the partner of the receiver should count as a point for the server.

_____69. Shortening your grip will aid in controlling the low to high drop shots.

_____70. All drop shots should land as close to the net as possible.

_____71. The basic grip for serving is the Eastern forehand grip.

_____72. You should attempt to hit your short service so the shuttle lands in the center of the opponent's receiving court, but to his/her backhand.

_____73. Deception is of little use when serving.

_____74. When attempting to generate force in stroking, the sequence to use is weight shift, hip rotation, shoulder rotation, arm extension and forearm rotation, in that order.

_____75. Points are ONLY scored by the serving side in badminton.

PART II: COMPLETION. Complete the following using the correct word from the text.

The projectile in badminton is the shuttlecock. It is generally called a _____ or _____. Badminton is an ancient game originating in _____ over 2,000 years ago. A children's game, very similar to badminton, was played in Europe in the 14th century. This game is called _____. The name "Poona" came from _____. It was in this country that British officers learned the game and brought it to England. The game was played at the country estate of the Duke of _____ in Gloucestershire, England, about the middle of the 19th century.

The first club for badminton in the United States was the _____ of _____. This club is recognized as the oldest badminton club in the world and is still in existence.

International competition for men takes place with the _____ competition. A similar tournament, called the _____, is held for women. These tournaments are held every _____ years. Although the U. S. was successful in winning the first three championships, it is now recognized that the best players in the world come from _____ and _____.

PART III: DEFINE THE FOLLOWING TERMS.

1. Block:

2. Unsight:

3. Hand Out:

4. Inning:

5. Setting:

6. Carry:

7. Balk:

8. Flick:

9. I.B.F.:

10. Let:

11. Pronation:

12. Rally:

13. Wood Shot:

14. Match:

15. Mixed Doubles:

PART IV: COMPLETION

There are six lines on a regulation badminton court. In the space provided below, name these lines.

List the parts of a badminton racket in the space below.

REFERENCES

Books

Bloss, Margaret Varner, *Badminton,* Fourth Edition, Wm. C. Brown Company, Dubuque, Iowa, 1971.

Davidson, Ken and Leo Gustavson, *Winning Badminton,* The Ronald Press, New York, New York, 1964.

Davis, Pat, *Badminton Complete,* A. S. Barnes and Company, Inc., Cranbury, New Jersey, 1967.

Pelton, Barry C., *Badminton,* Prentice-Hall, Inc., Englewood Cliffs, New Jersey, 1971.

Poole, James, *Badminton,* Goodyear Publishing Company, Pacific Palisades, California, 1969.

Rogers, Wynn, *Advanced Badminton,* Wm. C. Brown Company, Dubuque, Iowa, 1970.

Magazines and Guides

"Badminton Rules," United States Badminton Association, P.O. Box 237, Swartz Creek, Michigan 48473.

Badminton USA, Official Publication of the United States Badminton Association, P.O. Box 237, Swartz Creek, Michigan 48473.

Tennis-Badminton Guide, NAGWS-AAHPERD, 1201 16th Street NW, Washington, DC 20036.

"First Lessons in Badminton," June Day, *Journal of Health Physical Education and Recreation,* March 1963.

Official Handbook, American Badminton Association, 20 Warmesit Road, Waban, Massachusetts.